Brave in the Chaos

52 week study bible for black women
Transform Your Life by Overcoming Anxiety, Finding
Peace, and Trusting in God.

SARAH BENNETT

Contents:

This Book Belongs to:

_____

_____

How to Use This Book

This guide will help you make the most of each week's content, designed to alleviate anxiety and nurture your spirit. Each week, you'll explore a theme, engage with carefully curated Bible passages and readings, reflect on personal insights from the author, and draw inspiration from the stories of Black women of faith. Let's walk through the components you'll find in each week and how they can help you manage anxiety and strengthen your faith.

Weekly Theme:

- Each week begins with a Weekly Theme that sets the focus for your spiritual journey. This theme addresses common sources of anxiety and provides a foundation for the week's reflections and activities.

Biblical Passage of Calm:

- Start your week with a Biblical Passage of Calm, a short scripture specifically chosen to align with the weekly theme. This passage is designed to bring you immediate peace and help you center your mind and spirit, setting a calming tone for the days ahead.

Week's Readings:

- Engage with Week's Readings, which consist of seven daily Bible readings related to the theme. These readings provide a continuous source of spiritual nourishment and stress relief, helping you stay grounded and focused on God's word throughout the week.

Week's Reflection:

- Reflect on the Week's Reflection, a brief insight shared by the author, Sarah Bennett. These reflections are deeply personal and draw from Sarah's extensive research and experience, offering you practical ways to connect with the theme and manage your anxiety.

Reflections on the Week's Readings:

- Delve into the Reflections on the Week's Readings, where Sarah Bennett provides concise, clear, yet profound and practical insights for each day's reading. These reflections help you internalize the scriptures and apply their lessons to your daily life, offering concrete steps to alleviate anxiety.

Black Women of the Week:

- Be inspired by the Black Woman of the Week, a story of a Black woman who has overcome obstacles through faith. These stories provide hope, encouragement, and a reminder that you are not alone in your struggles. They showcase real-life examples of faith in action, empowering you to face your own challenges with confidence.

Week's Prayer:

- Connect with God through the Week's Prayer, a heartfelt prayer related to the weekly theme, crafted by Sarah Bennett. This prayer offers spiritual support and encouragement, helping you draw strength from God's presence and reinforcing your journey towards peace.

Reflective Questions:

- Engage with Reflective Questions, thoughtfully designed to guide your self-reflection on the week's readings and the story of the Black woman of the week. These questions deepen your understanding of the scriptures and the themes, helping you apply their messages to your life and further alleviate anxiety.

Introduction

Welcome to a transformative journey crafted with your unique needs in mind. This book is designed specifically for Black women seeking to ease anxiety and stress through the comforting embrace of God's Word. Drawing from "Research and Theory Religion and Spirituality in Coping With Stress", I, Sarah Bennett, have carefully studied this research to guide and shape the reflections and practices in this book.

Throughout this journey, you'll encounter inspiring stories from remarkable Black women who have harnessed biblical teachings to navigate their own challenges. Their experiences will resonate with you, offering both wisdom and encouragement.

Each week features thoughtfully selected scriptures meant to uplift and comfort during difficult times. You'll find practical challenges to help integrate faith into your daily life, along with original prayers designed to deepen your connection with God. These elements aim to provide personal strength and reflection.

Additionally, reflective journaling prompts and self-assessment questions are included to encourage a deeper exploration of your faith. This holistic approach combines inspiration, education, and spiritual motivation, helping you find peace and resilience.

May this book be a cherished companion on your journey, supporting you in embracing God's promises and discovering a profound sense of serenity through His presence. We hope it inspires and empowers you to build a legacy of faith that uplifts both you and those around you.

Week 1

Strength in Adversity

"The Lord is my strength and my shield; my heart
trusts in him, and he helps me."
Psalm 28:7

Readings:

Day 1: Exodus 14:14
Day 2: 2 Corinthians 12:9
Day 3: Isaiah 40:29
Day 4: Psalm 18:2
Day 5: Philippians 4:13
Day 6: Psalm 34:17
Day 7: Romans 15:13

Week's Reflection

In times of adversity, we find our strength and shield in the Lord. His power is perfected in our weakness, providing us with the strength needed to overcome any challenge and find peace through His constant support.

Reflections

Day 1: Exodus 14:14 assures us that God is always fighting on our behalf, even when we feel overwhelmed. Instead of succumbing to fear, let His promise of protection bring you peace and reassurance.

Day 2: 2 Corinthians 12:9 shows us that our vulnerabilities allow Christ's power to shine through. Embrace your weaknesses, and you'll find God's strength perfectly filling your life with grace and support.

Day 3: Isaiah 40:29 reminds us that God renews our strength when we're weary. His grace revitalizes us, offering comfort and a safe haven when we need it most, bringing hope and endurance.

Day 4: Psalm 18:2 tells us that God is our steadfast rock and safe refuge. Even in tough times, we can rely on His strength and protection, knowing He is our reliable savior and guide.

Day 5: Philippians 4:13 empowers us to overcome any challenge through Christ. His strength transforms our weaknesses into opportunities, showing His glory through our journey and triumphs.

Day 6: Psalm 34:17 reassures us that God hears our cries in times of trouble. He responds with deliverance, bringing relief and serenity, ensuring that our prayers are met with His comforting presence.

Day 7: Romans 15:13 encourages us to find joy and peace in the hope God offers. His Holy Spirit fills us with renewed confidence and hope, guiding us through adversity with strengthened faith.

(Black Women of the Week)

Sojourner Truth

Sojourner Truth, born Isabella Baumfree in 1797, was an extraordinary abolitionist and women's rights activist. Rooted in a deep faith in God, she endured the harsh realities of slavery until she escaped with her infant daughter in 1826, trusting in divine guidance for her freedom. After securing her release, she changed her name to Sojourner Truth, symbolizing her God-given mission to travel and speak out against injustice. In 1851, she delivered her renowned speech "Ain't I a Woman?" at the Ohio Women's Rights Convention, where she boldly confronted racial and gender biases, drawing strength from her faith. Her speech underscored her belief that God empowered her as a Black woman to challenge societal norms and advocate for the rights of all women. Sojourner's unwavering faith, combined with her powerful oratory, made her a pivotal figure in both the abolitionist and women's rights movements. Her legacy serves as a testament to the profound impact of faith in the fight against oppression, inspiring future generations to continue pursuing justice and human rights.

6

Lord, as we reflect on strength in adversity, we ask You to grant us the same courage and faith that Sojourner Truth displayed in her struggles. Strengthen our hearts and affirm Yourself as our shield and help in every challenge. Amen.

Reflective Questions

How can you experience and apply the strength God offers in your daily life, especially when facing anxieties and personal challenges?

....

....

....

....

....

....

....

....

....

....

Sojourner Truth used her voice to challenge injustices and showcase her strength. How can you draw inspiration from her life to confront your own challenges with courage and determination?

....

....

....

....

....

....

....

....

Week 2

Faith Against Odds

"Now faith is the substance of things hoped for, the
evidence of things not seen."
Hebrews 11:1

Readings:

Day 1: Isaiah 41:10

Day 2: Romans 8:28

Day 3: Psalm 46:1

Day 4: Hebrews 11:6

Day 5: 2 Corinthians 5:7

Day 6: Philippians 4:6-7

Day 7: Matthew 17:20

Week's Reflection

Faith in times of difficulty reminds us that, like the substance of what is hoped for and the evidence of what is not seen, God is with us, strengthening our hope and guiding us through seemingly insurmountable challenges.

Reflections

Day 1: Isaiah 41:10 reassures us that God is holding us close, even in our darkest times. His presence is our safe haven, providing the strength and comfort we need when everything feels uncertain.

Day 2: Romans 8:28 reminds us that every challenge we face is part of God's greater plan for our good. Trust that even trials are working together for your benefit and His divine purpose.

Day 3: Psalm 46:1 encourages us to find our refuge and strength in God. He is our unwavering support during life's difficulties, offering us peace and security no matter the troubles we face.

Day 4: Hebrews 11:6 highlights that faith is crucial in our relationship with God. By approaching Him with faith, we open ourselves to His guidance and the promises He has for us, even when we can't see them.

Day 5: 2 Corinthians 5:7 urges us to live by faith, not by what we see. This perspective allows us to face life's challenges with hope and assurance, knowing that faith provides the strength to persevere.

Day 6: Philippians 4:6-7 invites us to bring our worries to God through prayer and gratitude. In return, He offers a peace that transcends all understanding, guarding our hearts and minds in His comforting embrace.

Day 7: Matthew 17:20 teaches that faith, even as small as a mustard seed, has the power to overcome great obstacles. With faith, what seems impossible can become possible, transforming our lives in remarkable ways.

(Black Women of the Week)

Harriet Tubman

Harriet Tubman was born in 1822 in Maryland into slavery. Despite the abuses and hardships of slavery, Tubman developed an unshakable faith in God, which fueled her belief in freedom for herself and her fellow slaves. In 1849, guided by her faith, she escaped and freed herself from slavery. Yet, instead of enjoying her freedom, she chose to risk her life to help others achieve theirs, trusting in divine protection. Tubman became one of the most prominent leaders of the Underground Railroad, a secret network of routes and safe houses that helped slaves escape to free states and Canada. Over the course of more than a dozen missions, Harriet guided over 70 slaves to freedom, relying on her faith and courage to evade slave catchers. Her deep belief in God's guidance led her to face extreme dangers, knowing she was on a divine mission. Her life stands as a testament to how faith and determination can challenge and overcome the greatest adversities.

Lord, as we reflect on stories of liberation and faith, strengthen our confidence to face our anxieties and challenges. May we, like Harriet Tubman and the heroes of faith, find Your power in the midst of our struggles. Amen.

How can you apply the faith described in Hebrews 11:1 to a current situation of anxiety you are facing? What practical steps can you take to trust in the evidence of the unseen?

....
....
....
....
....
....
....
....
....

Harriet Tubman demonstrated exceptional courage in facing enormous risks for the freedom of others. How can you channel that same bravery in your life to confront your own challenges and anxieties?

....
....
....
....
....
....
....
....

Week 3

Hope in Despair

"For I know the plans I have for you, declares the Lord, plans to prosper you and not to harm you, plans to give you hope and a future."

Jeremiah 29:11

Readings:

Day 1: Psalm 42:5
Day 2: Romans 15:13
Day 3: Lamentations 3:22
Day 4: Isaiah 41:10
Day 5: 2 Corinthians 4:8-9
Day 6: Matthew 11:28
Day 7: Hebrews 10:23

Week's Reflection

In times of despair, hope in God offers us comfort and renewed strength. Through His faithfulness and promises, we can find peace and confidence to overcome any challenge and build a future filled with hope.

Reflections

Day 1: Psalm 42:5 encourages us not to let despair take over. Even in our low moments, we should lift our hope to God, who is our source of salvation and a reason for praise.

Day 2: Romans 15:13 reminds us that God fills us with hope, joy, and peace. Through His Holy Spirit, we stay hopeful and resilient, even when facing tough times.

Day 3: Lamentations 3:22-23 shows us God's unending faithfulness. Each new morning brings fresh mercies, ensuring His love and support are always with us, no matter how challenging our days may be.

Day 4: Isaiah 41:10 assures us that we're never alone in our struggles. God's presence provides constant strength and support, empowering us to face any challenge with confidence.

Day 5: 2 Corinthians 4:8-9 teaches us that even amid trials, we are not defeated. God upholds us and keeps us steadfast, helping us remain resilient despite adversity.

Day 6: Matthew 11:28 invites us to give our burdens to Jesus. He offers rest and relief, providing peace and comfort to our weary hearts and souls.

Day 7: Hebrews 10:23 urges us to firmly hold on to our hope in God's promises. His unwavering faithfulness provides the assurance we need for our future.

(Black Women of the Week)

Maya Angelou

Maya Angelou, born Marguerite Ann Johnson in 1928, was a poet and civil rights activist of great impact. Overcoming a childhood marked by trauma and discrimination, Angelou relied on her faith in God to find her voice through writing and poetry. Her autobiography, I Know Why the Caged Bird Sings, highlights her resilience and ability to find hope and strength in the face of adversity, drawing deeply from her spiritual beliefs. During the 1960s, she worked alongside civil rights leaders like Martin Luther King Jr. and Malcolm X, her faith guiding her as she used personal experiences to inspire others and advocate for meaningful social change. In addition to being a talented writer, Angelou was an actress, singer, and dancer, showcasing her artistic versatility, all of which she credited to her spiritual grounding. Her legacy lives on through her words and her courage, demonstrating how faith and hope can flourish even in the darkest times. Through her life and work, Maya Angelou remains a source of inspiration and a symbol of the fight for equality and justice.

Lord, in times of despair, we thank You for the hope You offer us. Just as Maya Angelou did and in every promise You make, strengthen our hearts to trust in Your plan and find peace in Your faithfulness. Amen.

Reflective Questions

How can you apply the hope and promise of God's faithfulness in your daily life, especially in moments of uncertainty and anxiety?

....
....
....
....
....
....
....
....
....
....

Maya Angelou transformed her difficult experiences into a message of hope and strength. What lessons can you learn from her life to maintain hope amid your own challenges?

....
....
....
....
....
....
....
....

Week 4

Courage to Overcome

"Be strong and courageous. Do not be afraid; do not be discouraged, for the Lord your God will be with you wherever you go."

Joshua 1:9

Readings:

Day 1: Isaiah 41:10
Day 2: 2 Timothy 1:7
Day 3: Psalm 27:1
Day 4: Joshua 1:7
Day 5: Exodus 14:14
Day 6: Psalm 31:24
Day 7: Romans 8:31

Week's Reflection

The profound lesson of this week is "Courage to Overcome". Just as God instructed Joshua to be strong and courageous, He reminds us that His presence provides the courage we need to face any challenge and overcome adversity.

Reflections

Day 1: Isaiah 41:10 God assures us of His presence and strength in our moments of weakness. He calls us to trust in His power to uphold and support us through every difficult situation.

Day 2: 2 Timothy 1:7 The Spirit God gives us is not one of fear, but of power and love. It empowers us to face challenges with courage and self-control, reflecting His strength within us.

Day 3: Psalm 27:1 When we feel afraid, the Lord is our light and salvation. His presence dispels fear and strengthens us to face any situation with confidence and faith.

14

Day 4: Joshua 1:7 Courage and effort are essential to living according to God's commandments. With His help, we can remain steadfast and brave in fulfilling His will.

Day 5: Exodus 14:14 God fights our battles and offers us peace. In the midst of conflict, we can rest assured that He is by our side, fighting for us.

Day 6: Psalm 31:24 Hope in the Lord gives us strength and encouragement. Even when facing difficulties, our trust in God sustains us and renews our spirit.

Day 7: Romans 8:31 With God by our side, no obstacle is insurmountable. His presence is our greatest assurance of success in the face of any adversity.

(Black Women of the Week)

Rosa Parks

Rosa Parks, born on February 4, 1913, in Tuskegee, Alabama, became a symbol of the civil rights movement, grounded in her faith in God. On December 1, 1955, in Montgomery, Alabama, Parks refused to give up her seat on a bus to a white man, drawing strength from her faith as she defied the segregation laws of the time. This courageous act of civil disobedience, guided by her belief in divine justice, sparked the Montgomery Bus Boycott, a pivotal movement in the fight for civil rights that eventually led to the desegregation of buses in the city. Known as "the mother of the civil rights movement," Parks dedicated her life to fighting racial injustice, driven by her deep religious conviction. Her bravery, rooted in her unwavering faith, continues to inspire many to persevere despite obstacles. Rosa Parks demonstrated that with faith, a single act of courage can change the course of history, leaving a lasting legacy in the struggle for justice and equality. 15

Lord, as we reflect on Your promise to be with us every step of the way, inspire us to find the courage to overcome our difficulties, just as Rosa Parks did with bravery and faith. May Your presence strengthen and guide us. Amen.

Reflective Questions

How can the reminder that God is with us at all times help us confront our fears and everyday challenges?

....
....
....
....
....
....
....
....
....
....

What can we learn from Rosa Parks' courage to face our own battles and remain steadfast in our convictions despite adversity?

....
....
....
....
....
....
....
....

Week 5

Joy in Suffering

"Consider it pure joy, my brothers and sisters, whenever
you face trials of many kinds."
James 1:2

Readings:

Day 1: Romans 5:3-4
Day 2: 1 Peter 1:6-7
Day 3: 2 Corinthians 4:17
Day 4: James 1:12
Day 5: Matthew 5:10
Day 6: Hebrews 12:2
Day 7: Psalm 30:5

Week's Reflection

This week's theme is "Joy in Suffering". It reminds us that trials and suffering can be transformed into moments of joy and growth, as God works through them to strengthen our faith and character.

Reflections

Day 1: Romans 5:3-4 Tribulations are not in vain; they produce patience and a strengthened faith. Each challenge is an opportunity to grow in character and hope in God.

Day 2: 1 Peter 1:6-7 Trials, though difficult, are temporary and serve a divine purpose. Tested faith reveals an eternal glory that surpasses any momentary suffering.

Day 3: 2 Corinthians 4:17 Our sufferings are light compared to the future glory God has in store for us. Each trial prepares us for a greater blessing.

Day 4: James 1:12 Perseverance in temptation leads to the promised reward. Our suffering has an eternal purpose and will be rewarded with the life God offers.

Day 5: Matthew 5:10 Suffering for the sake of righteousness is a sign of blessing. Although it is painful, it assures us a place in the kingdom of heaven.

Day 6: Hebrews 12:2 Jesus faced suffering for the joy of our salvation. Like Him, we can find joy in trials by focusing on the eternal reward.

Day 7: Psalm 30:5 Sorrow and suffering are temporary, but God's favor and the joy He offers are everlasting. The morning brings hope and renewal.

(Black Women of the Week)

Fannie Lou Hamer

Fannie Lou Hamer, born on October 6, 1917, in Mound Bayou, Mississippi, became a powerful voice in the civil rights movement, driven by her unwavering faith in God. Her life changed dramatically in 1962 when, after attempting to register to vote, she was arrested and brutally beaten in a Mississippi jail. This act of violence did not deter her; instead, it deepened her spiritual resolve and transformed her into a fervent activist. Guided by her faith, Hamer advocated for voting rights and fought against racial oppression. She helped to found the Student Nonviolent Coordinating Committee (SNCC) and the Mississippi Freedom Democratic Party, boldly challenging segregationist laws with divine conviction. Her famous speech at the 1964 Democratic National Convention, where she recounted the brutal racism she faced, underscored her courage and faith-driven determination. She dedicated her life to the struggle for social justice, and her legacy continues to inspire many to pursue equality and dignity, even in the face of suffering. Fannie Lou Hamer demonstrated that faith, perseverance, and courage can change the course of history, leaving an indelible mark on the fight for civil rights.

18

Lord, as we face our trials, help us find joy and strength in You, just as Fannie Lou Hamer did with her unwavering courage and faith. May our struggles bring us closer to Your purpose and grace. Amen.

Reflective Questions

How can you find joy in the midst of your current trials, and what role does faith play in transforming these difficulties into opportunities for spiritual growth?

....

....

....

....

....

....

....

....

....

....

How does Fannie Lou Hamer's courage inspire you to face your own challenges and persevere in your pursuit of justice and dignity, despite the difficulties you encounter?

....

....

....

....

....

....

....

Week 6

Wisdom in Decision Making

"If any of you lacks wisdom, let him ask of God, who gives to all liberally and without reproach, and it will be given to him."
James 1:5

Readings:

Day 1: Proverbs 2:6
Day 2: James 1:5
Day 3: Proverbs 3:5-6
Day 4: Psalm 32:8
Day 5: Proverbs 4:7
Day 6: Isaiah 11:2
Day 7: Luke 21:15

Week's Reflection

Wisdom in decision-making is crucial. God generously offers wisdom to those who seek it. Through faith and prayer, we can make decisions aligned with His will and face uncertainty with confidence.

Reflections

Day 1: Proverbs 2:6 God is the source of all true wisdom. By seeking His guidance, we gain the knowledge needed to make wise decisions and live with purpose.

Day 2: James 1:5 God is willing to grant us wisdom without reservation. By asking Him, we trust in His generosity and open ourselves to receiving divine direction in our choices.

Day 3: Proverbs 3:5-6 Trusting in God and acknowledging His guidance in our lives leads us on the right path. Our human prudence is limited compared to His infinite wisdom.

Day 4: Psalm 32:8 God promises to guide us and teach us the right path. By being attentive to His direction, we can make wise decisions and avoid mistakes.

Day 5: Proverbs 4:7 Wisdom should be our priority. By investing in acquiring it, we equip ourselves to face challenges with intelligence and discernment.

Day 6: Isaiah 11:2 The spirit of wisdom is essential for correct discernment. By seeking the guidance of the Holy Spirit, we receive the counsel and knowledge needed for our decisions.

Day 7: Luke 21:15 God provides us with wisdom and words that cannot be challenged. With His help, we can face and overcome opposition with confidence and clarity.

Coretta Scott King

Coretta Scott King, born on April 27, 1927, was a tireless leader of the civil rights movement, profoundly guided by her faith in God. Her life became intertwined with that of her husband, Martin Luther King Jr., with whom she shared the vision of a just society. After Martin's assassination in 1968, Coretta, relying on her deep spiritual conviction, continued the fight for equality and human rights with unwavering strength and determination. She founded the Martin Luther King Jr. Center for Nonviolent Social Change, using her faith as a foundation to preserve her husband's legacy and promote justice. Throughout her life, she faced personal and professional challenges with wisdom, courage, and divine guidance, demonstrating a steadfast faith in positive change. Her work left a lasting impact on the civil rights struggle, and her legacy continues to inspire women to approach their own choices with wisdom and bravery. Coretta Scott King showed that even in the midst of pain and adversity, faith and dedication to justice can transform lives and entire societies.

Lord, as we seek Your wisdom in our decisions, grant us the courage and clarity demonstrated by leaders like Coretta Scott King. May Your divine guidance enable us to make wise choices and walk in faith with each step we take. Amen.

Reflective Questions

How can you apply divine wisdom to your daily decisions, and in which areas of your life do you need to ask God for more clarity and direction?

....
....
....
....
....
....
....
....
....
....

How does Coretta Scott King's perseverance and wisdom inspire you in your own decisions and challenges, and what can you learn from her example to face your own trials with faith and courage?

....
....
....
....
....
....
....
....

Week 7

Peace in Turmoil

"Peace I leave with you; my peace I give you. I do not give to you as the world gives. Do not let your hearts be troubled and do not be afraid."
John 14:27

Readings:

Day 1: Isaiah 26-3
Day 2: Philippians 4:6-7
Day 3: Psalm 34:14
Day 4: John 16:33
Day 5: 2 Thessalonians 3:16
Day 6: Psalm 29:11
Day 7: Romans 15:13

Week's Reflection

True peace comes from God, not from the world. In times of turmoil, His peace sustains us and calms our hearts. By trusting in Him, we can face our anxieties with serenity and hope.

Reflections

Day 1: Isaiah 26-3 God promises perfect peace to those who remain focused on Him. His peace is a refuge amid distress, providing stability and calm in times of uncertainty.

Day 2: Philippians 4:6-7 The peace of God surpasses our human understanding. By presenting our concerns to Him with gratitude, we find a peace that guards our hearts and minds during difficult times.

Day 3: Psalm 34:14 Seeking and pursuing peace is a divine calling. Turning away from evil and doing good brings us closer to the peace God desires for us, helping us face adversity with calm.

Day 4: John 16:33 Jesus warns us that we will face challenges, but His victory over the world gives us peace. In Him, we find comfort and strength to overcome tribulations.

Day 5: 2 Thessalonians 3:16 God, as the Lord of peace, can grant us peace in every circumstance. His presence offers tranquility amidst difficulties, assuring us that we are never alone.

Day 6: Psalm 29:11 God provides strength and peace to His people. His blessing empowers us and grants the peace we need to confront challenges with confidence and serenity.

Day 7: Romans 15:13 The God of hope fills us with joy and peace in our faith. Through the Holy Spirit, we experience abundant hope and a peace that accompanies us at every moment.

Ida B. Wells

Ida B. Wells, born on July 16, 1862, was a courageous journalist and civil rights activist whose faith in God fueled her relentless fight against lynching. Her fearless investigations and publications, guided by her spiritual conviction, exposed racial brutality and challenged injustice during a time of great oppression. Despite facing threats and violence, Wells relied on her faith to remain steadfast in her mission to seek the truth and promote equality. She co-founded the first association of African American women, the National Association of Colored Women, and was an unwavering advocate for civil rights and women's suffrage, driven by her divine belief in justice. Her exemplary life demonstrates how faith, courage, and determination can bring peace and justice amidst turmoil and suffering. Wells also played a crucial role in founding the National Association for the Advancement of Colored People (NAACP), leaving a legacy that continues to inspire generations to pursue justice with integrity and bravery. Ida B. Wells' dedication to truth and social justice, underpinned by her faith, has left an indelible mark on the history of civil rights.

Lord, as we seek Your peace amid life's storms, strengthen us with the serenity that Jesus offered and the courage exemplified by Ida B. Wells. May Your peace surround and guide us in our moments of uncertainty. Amen.

Reflective Questions

How can you experience and maintain God's peace in the midst of your current concerns and anxieties, and what practices could help you trust more in His promise of peace?

....
....
....
....
....
....
....
....
....

How does the courage and commitment of Ida B. Wells inspire you to face your own challenges and anxieties, and how can you apply her example of striving for justice in your daily life?

....
....
....
....
....
....
....
....

Week 8

Love in Action

"Let all that you do be done in love."
1 Corinthians 16:14

Readings:

Day 1: 1 John 4:7
Day 2: Romans 13:10
Day 3: 1 Corinthians 13:4
Day 4: Ephesians 4:32
Day 5: Galatians 5:13
Day 6: John 15:12
Day 7: Colossians 3:14

Week's Reflection

Love in action is evident in our daily deeds. By loving others as God loves us, we reflect His true love, which transforms our lives and relationships, filling us with peace and purpose.

Reflections

Day 1: 1 John 4:7 Love is the foundation of our relationship with God and with others. Loving connects us with the divine essence and guides us to live in unity and understanding.

Day 2: Romans 13:10 Love is the cornerstone of fulfilling God's law. By loving our neighbor, we live in obedience and reflect divine goodness in our actions.

Day 3: 1 Corinthians 13:4-5 True love is patient and kind. It doesn't seek harm or become consumed by ego. It calls us to act with humility and avoid holding onto grudges.

26

Day 4: Ephesians 4:32 Being kind and forgiving is essential for maintaining healthy relationships. God's love compels us to act with compassion and forgive as He has forgiven us.

Day 5: Galatians 5:13 Freedom in Christ calls us to serve others with love. We should use our freedom not for personal gain but to help and love others.

Day 6: John 15:12 Jesus commands us to love as He has loved us: without reservation and with total commitment. This love challenges us to sacrifice our own interests for the good of others.

Day 7: Colossians 3:14 Love is the perfect bond that unites all virtues. By clothing ourselves in love, our actions and relationships reflect the perfection of God's goodness and peace.

Marian Anderson

Marian Anderson, born on February 27, 1897, was an African American soprano whose voice captivated the world, fueled by her deep faith in God. Despite facing racism and exclusion, her spiritual strength and dignity helped her break down barriers. In 1939, her performance at the Lincoln Memorial, after being denied access to Constitution Hall because of her race, became a milestone in the civil rights movement, driven by her unwavering belief in divine justice. Anderson not only shone on the international stage but also used her faith-inspired fame to advocate for equality and justice. Her courage and dedication, grounded in her spiritual convictions, demonstrated how love and perseverance can turn adversity into opportunities for social change. In addition to her historic performance, Anderson became the first African American to sing at the Metropolitan Opera in New York in 1955, marking another crucial moment in civil rights history. Her life continues to inspire all to pursue their dreams and stand up for what is right, showing that faith and true love in action can change the world. Marian Anderson's story is a testament to the power of music, faith, and the human spirit to overcome barriers and promote social justice.

27

Lord, as we reflect on Your call to love in action and follow Marian Anderson's example, may we live each day with true love, reflecting Your grace in our actions and lives. Amen.

How can you integrate love into your daily actions so that every aspect of your life aligns with the love God has commanded, and what changes could you make to reflect that love in your relationships and activities?

....
....
....
....
....
....
....
....
....

How does Marian Anderson's example inspire you to act with love and courage in your own life, especially in overcoming adversity and advocating for justice and equality?

....
....
....
....
....
....
....
....

Week 9

Healing through Faith

"He heals the brokenhearted and binds up their wounds."
Psalm 147:3

Readings:

Day 1: Matthew 11:28
Day 2: Psalm 34:18
Day 3: Isaiah 41:10
Day 4: Jeremiah 30:17
Day 5: 1 Peter 5:7
Day 6: Philippians 4:6-7
Day 7: Isaiah 53:5

Week's Reflection

Healing through faith reveals that God has the power to heal our emotional and physical wounds. By trusting in Him, we find peace and restoration amidst our anxieties and concerns.

Reflections

Day 1: Matthew 11:28 Jesus invites us to find rest in Him. His promise of relief and rest is a safe refuge for our weary and anxious souls.

Day 2: Psalm 34:18 God is near to those with broken hearts. His presence brings comfort and hope, reminding us that we are not alone in our struggles.

Day 3: Isaiah 41:10 We need not fear because God is with us. His strength and constant support sustain us, giving us the confidence to face any challenge.

Day 4: Jeremiah 30:17 God promises healing for our wounds. His love and mercy restore us, giving us the chance to heal and renew ourselves.

Day 5: 1 Peter 5:7 We can place our anxieties in God's hands. He cares for us with love and provides the peace we need to address our concerns.

Day 6: Philippians 4:6-7 Prayer and gratitude draw us closer to God. His peace, which surpasses all understanding, guards our hearts and minds amidst anxiety.

Day 7: Isaiah 53:5 Jesus' work on the cross brings us healing. His sacrifice offers restoration and peace, assuring us that our wounds can be healed.

Mary McLeod Bethune

Mary McLeod Bethune, born July 10, 1875, was an educator and civil rights leader whose legacy endures to this day, deeply guided by her faith in God. The daughter of freed slaves, Bethune grew up in a time of great discrimination, but her spiritual conviction and determination led her to found Bethune-Cookman University in 1904, one of the foremost institutions for the education of African Americans. In addition to her educational work, she was a staunch advocate for civil rights and worked tirelessly to improve the conditions of African Americans, drawing strength from her faith. Her influence reached the White House, where she served as an advisor to President Franklin D. Roosevelt, inspired by her belief in divine justice. Bethune firmly believed in the power of education and community service as tools for social transformation, underpinned by her spiritual convictions. Her life is an inspiring testament to how faith and dedication can heal communities and pave the way to a better future.

30

Lord, as we reflect on Your healing power and the example of Mary McLeod Bethune, we ask that You fill us with faith and strength to overcome our anxieties and wounds. May we find peace and purpose in Your love and in our service to others. Amen.

Reflective Questions

How can you trust more in God to heal your emotional wounds and reduce your anxiety? What steps can you take to rest in His promise of healing and peace?

....
....
....
....
....
....
....
....
....

How does Mary McLeod Bethune's life inspire you to use your own gifts and talents to heal and transform your community? What concrete actions can you take to follow her example of service and dedication?

....
....
....
....
....
....
....

Week 10

Patience in Waiting

"But they that wait upon the Lord shall renew their strength; they shall mount up with wings as eagles; they shall run, and not be weary; and they shall walk, and not faint."

Isaiah 40:31

Readings:

Day 1: Psalm 27:14

Day 2: Lamentations 3:25

Day 3: Romans 8:25

Day 4: Psalm 37:7

Day 5: James 5:7-8

Day 6: Hebrews 10:36

Day 7: Galatians 6:9

Week's Reflection

Patience in waiting strengthens and renews us. By trusting in God's timing, we find hope and resilience, knowing that our anxieties and concerns are eased through His promise.

Reflections

Day 1: Psalm 27:14 Waiting on the Lord strengthens the heart. In times of anxiety, His presence fills us with courage and confidence.

Day 2: Lamentations 3:25-26 God is good to those who wait for Him. Patience in waiting brings a deep communion with His spirit.

Day 3: Romans 8:25 Hope in the unseen teaches us patience. Even if we don't see immediate results, faith in God sustains us.

32

Day 4: Psalm 37:7 Calmness and waiting on the Lord shield us from anxiety. Trusting in His justice brings us peace during times of distress.

Day 5: James 5:7-8 The patience of the farmer inspires us to wait with hope. Just as he waits for the harvest, we await the coming of the Lord.

Day 6: Hebrews 10:36 Patience is essential to receive God's promises. By doing His will, we strengthen our faith and anticipate His reward.

Day 7: Galatians 6:9 Let us not grow weary of doing good. Patience and perseverance in our good deeds will bring forth fruit in due time.

Phillis Wheatley

Phillis Wheatley, born in Africa in 1753 and brought to America as a slave, was the first African American woman to publish a book of poetry, a feat achieved through her profound faith in God. Despite the hardships she faced, her religious convictions and literary talent were recognized by her owners, who provided her with an education. In 1773, she published "Poems on Various Subjects, Religious and Moral," establishing herself as a prominent literary figure, guided by her spiritual beliefs. Wheatley used her poetry to express her experiences and Christian faith, addressing themes of freedom and humanity with divine inspiration. Her work challenged contemporary perceptions of the intellectual capabilities of African Americans, reflecting deep introspection and a strong connection to spiritual values. Her faith allowed her to connect with a diverse audience and earn admiration both in America and Europe. Throughout her life, Phillis Wheatley maintained unwavering faith and patience, becoming a symbol of resilience and hope. Her legacy continues to inspire generations to persevere and find strength in adversity, demonstrating that faith and determination can overcome the most difficult barriers.

Lord, as we reflect on Your promise to renew our strength and the example of patience shown by Phillis Wheatley, we ask You to give us the courage to wait on You with hope and faith. Help us to find peace in Your perfect timing. Amen.

Reflective Questions

How can you cultivate patience in your daily life as you wait on the Lord? What practices help you strengthen your faith and reduce anxiety?

....
....
....
....
....
....
....
....
....
....

How does Phillis Wheatley's life inspire you to persevere through your own challenges? In what ways can you use your talents and faith to overcome adversity and help others?

....
....
....
....
....
....
....
....

Week 11

Trust in God's Plan

"Trust in the Lord with all your heart and lean not on your
own understanding."
Proverbs 3:5

Readings:

Day 1: Jeremiah 29:11
Day 2: Psalm 37:5
Day 3: Romans 8:28
Day 4: Isaiah 55:8-9
Day 5: Proverbs 16:9
Day 6: Psalm 32:8
Day 7: 1 Peter 5:7

Week's Reflection

Trust in God's plan with all your heart. His wisdom surpasses ours, guiding us on the right path and relieving our anxieties and concerns.

Reflections

Day 1: Jeremiah 29:11 God has plans of peace and hope for us. Trusting in His purpose provides security in times of uncertainty.

Day 2: Psalm 37:5 Committing our path to the Lord ensures His guidance. Trusting in His plan frees us from stress and doubt.

Day 3: Romans 8:28 Everything works together for good for those who love God. Even amidst challenges, we can trust that He has a greater purpose.

Day 4: Isaiah 55:8-9 God's thoughts and ways are higher than ours. Trusting in His wisdom helps us accept what we do not understand.

Day 5: Proverbs 16:9 God directs our steps, even when we don't understand the path. His guidance is always toward our good.

Day 6: Psalm 32:8 The Lord instructs and guides us with love. Trusting in His oversight brings us peace in every step we take.

Day 7: 1 Peter 5:7 We can cast our anxieties on God. His care and love support us through every moment of concern.

Ella Baker

Ella Baker was a tireless advocate for civil and human rights in the United States, guided by her deep faith in God. Born on December 13, 1903, in Norfolk, Virginia, she dedicated her life to fighting against racial injustice and inequality, driven by her spiritual convictions. Baker worked alongside prominent leaders like Martin Luther King Jr. and played a pivotal role in organizing the Student Nonviolent Coordinating Committee (SNCC), which empowered young activists to take action, inspired by her belief in divine justice. She believed deeply in the power of grassroots leadership and the importance of listening to and amplifying the voices of the oppressed, viewing her work as a calling from God. Known for her behind-the-scenes efforts, Baker emphasized collective action over individual recognition. Throughout her life, she faced numerous challenges, but her unwavering faith in justice and her belief in a higher purpose kept her steadfast. Baker's commitment to the cause of equality and her ability to inspire others demonstrated her profound impact on the civil rights movement, illustrating how faith can guide our actions and give us the courage to persevere.

36

Lord, as we reflect on Your plan and the example of Ella Baker, we ask You to help us fully trust in Your guidance. Strengthen our faith and allow us to find peace in Your infinite wisdom. Amen.

Reflective Questions

How can you learn to trust more in God's plan in your daily life? What practical steps can you take to cast your anxieties on Him?

....
....
....
....
....
....
....
....
....
....

How does Ella Baker's life inspire you to act with faith and perseverance in the pursuit of justice? How can you apply her example in your own community and daily life?

....
....
....
....
....
....
....
....

Week 12

Gratitude in All Circumstances

"Give thanks in all circumstances; for this is God's
will for you in Christ Jesus."
1 Thessalonians 5:18

Readings:

Day 1: Philippians 4:6-7
Day 2: Psalm 100:4
Day 3: Colossians 3:15-17
Day 4: Psalm 107:1
Day 5: Ephesians 5:20
Day 6: 1 Chronicles 16:34
Day 7: Hebrews 12:28

Week's Reflection

Gratitude in all circumstances connects us to God's will and brings us peace. Recognizing His goodness in every situation, whether great or small, transforms our perspective and strengthens us.

Reflections

Day 1: Philippians 4:6-7 Gratitude in prayer brings a peace that surpasses all understanding, freeing our minds from anxiety.

Day 2: Psalm 100:4 Entering God's presence with thanksgiving opens our hearts to His love and blessings.

Day 3: Colossians 3:15-17 Gratitude and the message of Christ unite us in peace and guide us in wisdom and love.

Day 4: Psalm 107:1 Giving thanks to the Lord reminds us of His goodness and eternal love, strengthening our faith.

Day 5: Ephesians 5:20 Thanking God at all times keeps us connected to His will and His constant love.

Day 6: 1 Chronicles 16:34 Gratitude for God's eternal love fills us with hope and trust in His faithfulness.

Day 7: Hebrews 12:28 Receiving God's unshakable kingdom with gratitude inspires us to worship Him with reverence and awe.

Zora Neale Hurston

Zora Neale Hurston was a renowned author and anthropologist whose work profoundly impacted American literature and the study of African American culture, guided by her deep faith. Born on January 7, 1891, in Notasulga, Alabama, Hurston faced significant challenges throughout her life but emerged as a key figure of the Harlem Renaissance, drawing strength from her spiritual beliefs. Her most celebrated work, "Their Eyes Were Watching God," published in 1937, is a seminal novel that delves into themes of black identity, gender, and personal growth, reflecting her faith's influence on her exploration of personal and communal resilience. The book is notable for its rich portrayal of African American life and its innovative use of dialect and narrative style. In addition to her literary achievements, Hurston made substantial contributions to anthropology. Her extensive travels in the American South and the Caribbean, driven by her faith in preserving cultural heritage, allowed her to document folklore, customs, and oral histories of African American communities. Despite facing considerable adversity and periods of obscurity, Hurston's unwavering dedication to her craft and her commitment to representing black voices, fueled by her belief in a higher purpose, have left an enduring legacy. Her life and work continue to inspire, highlighting the significance of perseverance, cultural pride, and the transformative power of faith in storytelling. 39

Lord, as we reflect on gratitude and the example of Zora Neale Hurston, we ask You to help us recognize and give thanks for Your goodness in every circumstance. Strengthen our spirit to persevere and find peace in Your constant love. Amen.

Reflective Questions

How can you practice gratitude amid your daily challenges and recognize God's goodness in all circumstances?

....
....
....
....
....
....
....
....
....
....

How does Zora Neale Hurston's life inspire you to face your own challenges with gratitude and perseverance? What lessons from her story can you apply to your daily life?

....
....
....
....
....
....
....

Week 13

Faith in God's Timing

"He has made everything beautiful in its time."
Ecclesiastes 3:11

Readings:

Day 1: Isaiah 40:31
Day 2: Jeremiah 29:11
Day 3: Habakkuk 2:3
Day 4: Galatians 6:9
Day 5: Psalm 27:14
Day 6: Ecclesiastes 3:1
Day 7: Romans 8:28

Week's Reflection

Faith in God's timing teaches us to trust and wait patiently. He makes everything beautiful in His time, reminding us that His plan is perfect and leads us to a hopeful future.

Reflections

Day 1: Isaiah 40:31 Waiting on the Lord renews our strength and empowers us to continue, trusting in His perfect timing.

Day 2: Jeremiah 29:11 God's plans for us are filled with well-being and hope, even when we don't fully understand them.

Day 3: Habakkuk 2:3 Even if the vision seems delayed, we must wait with faith, knowing it will come to fruition in God's timing.

Day 4: Galatians 6:9 We should not grow weary of doing good, for the harvest will come at the right time.

Day 5: Psalm 27:14 Waiting on the Lord strengthens us and fills us with courage to face each day.

Day 6: Ecclesiastes 3:1 Everything has its time and season under heaven, guided by God's wisdom.

Day 7: Romans 8:28 God works all things for our good, fulfilling His purpose in our lives.

Shirley Chisholm

Shirley Chisholm was a groundbreaking politician and educator whose unwavering faith guided her remarkable journey. Born on November 30, 1924, in Brooklyn, New York, Chisholm faced numerous challenges but remained steadfast in her beliefs and her mission to bring about change. Elected to the U.S. Congress in 1968 as the first Black woman, her campaign slogan, "Unbought and Unbossed," reflected her commitment to justice, equality, and integrity. In 1972, she made history again by becoming the first Black woman to run for the U.S. presidency on a major party ticket. Though she did not win, her candidacy was a trailblazer that inspired many and paved the way for future leaders. Throughout her career, Chisholm's deep faith was evident in her fearless advocacy for education, health care, and workers' rights. Her legacy serves as a testament to the power of faith and determination in overcoming obstacles and advancing social justice. Shirley Chisholm's life continues to inspire generations, highlighting the transformative impact of faith and perseverance in the quest for equality and change. 42

Lord, as we reflect on the importance of faith in Your timing and the inspiring example of Shirley Chisholm, we ask You to help us wait with patience and trust in Your perfect plan. Strengthen our spirit and guide our steps. Amen.

Reflective Questions

How can you apply patience and faith in God's timing to your current circumstances and trust in His plan for your life?

....
....
....
....
....
....
....
....
....
....

How does Shirley Chisholm's life inspire you to persevere in your goals and trust that God has a perfect purpose for you?

....
....
....
....
....
....
....
....

Week 14

Resilience in Trials

"Not only so, but we also glory in our sufferings, because we know that suffering produces perseverance; perseverance, character; and character, hope."
Romans 5:3-4

Readings:

Day 1: James 1:2-3
Day 2: 1 Peter 5:10
Day 3: Isaiah 41:10
Day 4: 2 Corinthians 4:8-9
Day 5: Romans 8:18
Day 6: Psalm 34:19
Day 7: 1 Corinthians 10:13

Week's Reflection

Resilience in trials strengthens us and leads us to greater hope. Difficulties shape our character and teach us to trust in God's grace and perfect plan.

Reflections

Day 1: James 1:2-3 Trials strengthen our faith and teach us to be steadfast and firm in our trust in God.

Day 2: 1 Peter 5:10 God restores and strengthens us after trials, reminding us that our difficulties are temporary and His grace is eternal.

Day 3: Isaiah 41:10 We need not fear, for God is with us, strengthening and upholding us with His power.

Day 4: 2 Corinthians 4:8-9 Even though we face tribulations, we are not destroyed or abandoned; God sustains us in our struggles.

Day 5: Romans 8:18 Present sufferings pale in comparison to the future glory that God will reveal in us.

Day 6: Psalm 34:19 Despite many troubles, God promises to deliver us from them all, offering us hope and comfort.

Day 7: 1 Corinthians 10:13 God is faithful and will not allow us to face more than we can bear; He always provides a way out to endure.

Dr. Kizzmekia Corbett

Dr. Kizzmekia Corbett is a distinguished immunologist and vaccine developer whose faith played a crucial role in her accomplishments. Born in North Carolina in 1986, Corbett's passion for science and belief in her purpose drove her to excel academically, earning a degree in biology and a PhD in microbiology and immunology. Her groundbreaking work gained widespread recognition during the COVID-19 pandemic when she led the development of the Moderna vaccine at the National Institutes of Health (NIH). Corbett's expertise and unwavering faith were instrumental in creating a vaccine that saved countless lives worldwide. Beyond her scientific achievements, Corbett has broken barriers and challenged stereotypes in the field of science. Her journey is a testament to how faith in one's abilities and relentless effort can overcome significant obstacles. Her accomplishments inspire many, especially Black women, to pursue careers in STEM fields and believe in their potential to drive meaningful change. Dr. Corbett's story exemplifies how dedication and faith can profoundly impact global health and social progress.

Lord, as we reflect on resilience in trials and the inspiring example of Dr. Kizzmekia Corbett, we ask You to strengthen our faith and character amidst difficulties. Help us to trust in Your plan and persevere with hope. Amen.

Reflective Questions

How can you apply resilience in your daily life, especially when facing trials and challenges?

....
....
....
....
....
....
....
....
....
....

What lessons from Dr. Kizzmekia Corbett's life can you adopt to persevere in your own challenges and trust in your abilities?

....
....
....
....
....
....
....
....

Week 15

Joy in the Journey

"The joy of the Lord is your strength."
Nehemiah 8:10

Readings:

Day 1: Psalm 16:11
Day 2: Philippians 4:4
Day 3: Psalm 118:24
Day 4: Isaiah 55:12
Day 5: Romans 15:13
Day 6: Proverbs 17:22
Day 7: John 15:11

Week's Reflection

Joy in the Lord is our strength. Finding joy in every step of the journey helps us face challenges with hope and peace, knowing that God sustains us.

Reflections

Day 1: Psalm 16:11 God reveals the path of life to us and fills us with joy in His presence, granting us eternal delight.

Day 2: Philippians 4:4 Rejoicing in the Lord is a repeated command, reminding us to always find joy in His presence.

Day 3: Psalm 118:24 Each day is an opportunity to celebrate and find joy in the Lord's works.

Day 4: Isaiah 55:12 Joy and peace guide us, and creation itself joins in our joy in God.

Day 5: Romans 15:13 God fills us with joy and peace so that our hope in Him overflows through the Holy Spirit.

Day 6: Proverbs 17:22 A cheerful heart is healing and revitalizing, while a broken spirit drains our strength.

Day 7: John 15:11 Jesus gives us His joy so that our joy may be complete and full.

Oprah Winfrey

Oprah Winfrey, born on January 29, 1954, in Kosciusko, Mississippi, is a celebrated media executive, talk show host, and philanthropist. Despite a challenging upbringing marked by poverty and abuse, her unwavering faith and inner strength guided her to become one of the world's most influential figures. Oprah's rise to fame came through her transformative talk show, "The Oprah Winfrey Show," which aired from 1986 to 2011. The show was not only a platform for discussing critical social issues and personal development but also a reflection of her deep belief in spiritual growth and empowerment. In addition to her media achievements, Oprah's faith has driven her philanthropic work. She established the Oprah Winfrey Foundation and Oprah's Angel Network, focusing on education, community support, and social change. Her faith-inspired vision led to the creation of the Oprah Winfrey Foundation's Leadership Academy for Girls in South Africa, which provides educational opportunities for young women in need. Oprah's journey is a powerful example of how faith and resilience can overcome adversity and lead to extraordinary accomplishments. Her life illustrates how a deep commitment to personal and spiritual values can create meaningful change, both in individual lives and across communities.

Lord, as we reflect on joy in the journey and the inspiring example of Oprah Winfrey, we ask that You fill our hearts with Your joy and strength. Help us face challenges with hope and share that joy with others. Amen.

Reflective Questions

How can you find and maintain the joy of the Lord amid your own daily challenges?

....
....
....
....
....
....
....
....
....
....

What lessons from Oprah Winfrey's life can you adopt to face your own difficulties with joy and hope?

....
....
....
....
....
....
....

Week 16

Courage in the Face of Fear

"When I am afraid, I put my trust in you."
Psalm 56:3

Readings:

Day 1: Isaiah 41:10
Day 2: Joshua 1:9
Day 3: 2 Timothy 1:7
Day 4: Psalm 34:4
Day 5: Romans 8:15
Day 6: John 14:27
Day 7: Psalm 27:1

Week's Reflection

This week's profound theme is "Courage in the Face of Fear." When we trust in God during times of fear, we find the strength to confront our challenges, knowing we are not alone and that His presence upholds us.

Reflections

Day 1: Isaiah 41:10 God strengthens and helps us, assuring us that His presence supports us at all times.

Day 2: Joshua 1:9 Courage comes from knowing that God is with us every step of the way.

Day 3: 2 Timothy 1:7 God has given us a spirit of power, love, and self-discipline, not of fear.

Day 4: Psalm 34:4 Seeking the Lord in our fears results in deliverance and peace.

Day 5: Romans 8:15 As God's children, we are not enslaved by fear but can confidently cry out to our Father.

Day 6: John 14:27 The peace Jesus gives surpasses any fear or anxiety the world may offer.

Day 7: Psalm 27:1 With God as our light and salvation, there is nothing and no one that should intimidate us.

Claudette Colvin

Claudette Colvin, a pivotal figure in the civil rights movement, achieved historical significance at the age of 15 when she refused to give up her seat on a segregated bus in Montgomery, Alabama, in March 1955. This act of bravery, which preceded Rosa Parks' more widely known protest by nine months, was driven by her deep Christian faith and moral convictions. Despite her youth, Claudette's steadfast belief in equality and justice fueled her resistance against racial segregation. Her refusal to vacate her seat led to her arrest, becoming a key moment in the battle against segregation. Colvin's faith and courage played a crucial role in the legal actions that eventually dismantled segregation in Montgomery's public transportation system. Although her story was overshadowed by Parks' more famous protest, Colvin's steadfastness was fundamental in advancing the civil rights movement. Her life exemplifies how deep faith and unwavering conviction can inspire profound social change. Claudette Colvin's legacy highlights that meaningful progress often begins with acts of bravery and a commitment to justice, driven by a profound sense of moral purpose. 51

Lord, as we reflect on courage in adversity and the brave story of Claudette Colvin, we ask that You grant us the strength to face our own fears. May Your presence give us the courage to pursue justice and peace. Amen.

Reflective Questions

How can you apply courage and trust in God to situations of fear in your daily life?

....
....
....
....
....
....
....
....
....
....

What lessons from Claudette Colvin's bravery can you incorporate into your own struggle against injustice or fear?

....
....
....
....
....
....
....
....

Week 17

Love as a Foundation

"And now these three remain: faith, hope and love.
But the greatest of these is love."
1 Corinthians 13:13

Readings:

Day 1: 1 John 4:18
Day 2: Romans 8:38-39
Day 3: 1 Corinthians 16:14
Day 4: Colossians 3:14
Day 5: 1 Peter 4:8
Day 6: John 15:12
Day 7: Ephesians 5:2

Week's Reflection

This week's profound theme is "Love as a Foundation." Love is the bedrock of our faith and hope, it strengthens us in times of anxiety, and unites us in God's grace.

Reflections

Day 1: 1 John 4:18 God's perfect love removes fear, reminding us that we need not be afraid when enveloped in His love.

Day 2: Romans 8:38-39 Nothing can separate us from God's love in Christ, providing us with security and comfort in any circumstance.

Day 3: 1 Corinthians 16:14 Acting with love in all we do transforms our actions and relationships.

53

Day 4: Colossians 3:14 Love is the bond that perfects all virtues, uniting and strengthening our lives.

Day 5: 1 Peter 4:8 Deep and sincere love for others can cover and heal many wrongs and wounds.

Day 6: John 15:12 Loving others as Jesus loved us is the supreme command that guides our relationships.

Day 7: Ephesians 5:2 Living in love, following Christ's example, is an offering that pleases God and transforms our lives.

Michelle Obama

Michelle Obama, former First Lady of the United States, embodies the strength and guidance of faith in her journey. Born on January 17, 1964, in Chicago, she navigated and triumphed over numerous obstacles with unwavering belief and determination. With a law background, Michelle rose to prominence as an attorney and became a notable advocate for social issues. During her White House tenure, she championed initiatives such as "Let's Move!" to combat childhood obesity and "Let Girls Learn" to enhance educational opportunities for girls worldwide. Michelle Obama's genuine connection with people from diverse backgrounds has cemented her status as a cherished figure. Her memoir, "Becoming," explores her personal experiences, including her battles with anxiety, and underscores the significance of faith, family support, and community in her life. She has leveraged her platform to promote resilience, empowerment, and the transformative impact of education. Her narrative illustrates how faith, dedication, and perseverance can overcome adversity and inspire others to pursue their passions and effect meaningful change. 54

Lord, as we reflect on the power of love in our lives and the inspiring story of Michelle Obama, we ask You to help us love deeply and fearlessly. May Your love be the foundation of our actions and relationships. Amen.

Reflective Questions

How can you let God's love be the foundation of your daily actions and face anxiety with confidence?

....

....

....

....

....

....

....

....

....

....

What aspects of Michelle Obama's story inspire you to use love and dedication to overcome your own challenges?

....

....

....

....

....

....

....

....

Week 18

Wisdom from Above

"For the Lord gives wisdom; from his mouth come knowledge and understanding."
Proverbs 2:6

Readings:

Day 1: James 1:5
Day 2: Proverbs 3:13-14
Day 3: Ecclesiastes 2:26
Day 4: Proverbs 4:7
Day 5: Colossians 2:2-3
Day 6: Proverbs 8:11
Day 7: Job 12:13

Week's Reflection

This week's profound theme is "Wisdom from Above." It reminds us that true wisdom comes from God, offering clarity and peace even in moments of anxiety.

Reflections

Day 1: James 1:5 God gives wisdom generously to those who ask, reminding us that we can always turn to Him for guidance.

Day 2: Proverbs 3:13-14 Wisdom is more valuable than any material wealth, offering us a perspective that transcends the temporal.

Day 3: Ecclesiastes 2:26 God grants wisdom and joy to those who please Him, highlighting the importance of seeking His favor.

Day 4: Proverbs 4:7 Pursuing wisdom should be our top priority, as it is essential for living with understanding and discernment.

Day 5: Colossians 2:2-3 In Christ are hidden all the treasures of wisdom and knowledge, uniting our hearts in love and understanding.

Day 6: Proverbs 8:11 Wisdom surpasses any desire we might have, guiding us towards decisions and paths that honor God.

Day 7: Job 12:13 God is the source of all wisdom and power, and we can trust in His counsel and understanding in every situation.

Toni Morrison

Toni Morrison, born Chloe Ardelia Wofford on February 18, 1931, in Lorain, Ohio, is a towering figure in American literature and a Nobel Prize winner. Growing up in a family that embraced spiritual values and oral traditions, Morrison's deep faith influenced her narrative voice and storytelling approach. Her belief in the power of storytelling as a means of spiritual and cultural exploration guided her to become the first Black woman to win the Nobel Prize in Literature in 1993, marking a significant milestone in her career. Morrison's novels, including "Beloved," "Song of Solomon," and "The Bluest Eye," explore the complexities of African American life with rich, evocative prose. Her work delves into themes of faith, identity, and resilience, offering profound insights into the struggles and triumphs of Black Americans. Through her storytelling, Morrison illuminated the often overlooked experiences of marginalized communities, reflecting her belief in the transformative power of faith and narrative. Her literary genius and unwavering commitment to addressing spiritual and cultural truths have left an indelible mark on literature and society. Morrison's legacy is a powerful testament to how faith and storytelling can drive meaningful change and elevate the voices of the oppressed.

Lord, as we reflect on divine wisdom and the life of Toni Morrison, we ask You to guide us with Your wisdom and strengthen us in our struggles. May our words and actions reflect Your love and understanding. Amen.

Reflective Questions

How can you apply divine wisdom in your daily life to handle anxiety and concerns?

....
....
....
....
....
....
....
....
....
....

What lessons from Toni Morrison's life inspire you to seek and share the truth in your own life?

....
....
....
....
....
....
....
....

Week 19

Compassion for Others

"Be kind and compassionate to one another, forgiving each
other, just as in Christ God forgave you."
Ephesians 4:32

Readings:

Day 1: Luke 6:36
Day 2: Matthew 5:7
Day 3: Colossians 3:12
Day 4: Proverbs 19:17
Day 5: 1 John 3:17
Day 6: James 2:13
Day 7: Hebrews 13:16

Week's Reflection

This week's theme is "Compassion for Others." God calls us to be kind and compassionate, forgiving others as He has forgiven us, reflecting His love in our actions towards others.

Reflections

Day 1: Luke 6:36 Divine mercy calls us to act with compassion towards others, reflecting the character of our Heavenly Father in our daily interactions.

Day 2: Matthew 5:7 Mercy is a blessing that God promises to those who practice it, showing us that by being compassionate, we also receive His grace.

Day 3: Colossians 3:12 As God's chosen people, we should clothe ourselves with mercy, kindness, and humility, showing love and understanding in our relationships with others.

Day 4: Proverbs 19:17 Helping the poor is a way of lending to God, who will reward us for our acts of compassion and generosity.

Day 5: 1 John 3:17 Closing our hearts to the needs of others contradicts the love of God within us; we should let His love flow through our actions.

Day 6: James 2:13 Mercy triumphs over judgment, and by showing compassion, we avoid severe judgment, creating space for love and grace in our lives.

Day 7: Hebrews 13:16 God is pleased with our acts of kindness and mutual support, and these sacrifices of love and support are valuable in His eyes.

Ruby Bridges

Ruby Bridges became a beacon of courage and faith at just six years old when she integrated an all-white elementary school in the South in 1960. Born in Tylertown, Mississippi, in 1954, Ruby and her family moved to New Orleans, where her faith and resilience led her to make history. Confronted by hostility and protests, Ruby attended William Frantz Elementary School under the protection of federal marshals, guided by her devoted teacher, Barbara Henry, who embraced Ruby's presence despite the immense opposition. Ruby's faith in her mission and her unwavering belief in the importance of education were crucial during this turbulent period. Her bravery in overcoming racial hatred and discrimination highlighted her profound commitment to equality and education. Despite the intense challenges, Ruby's faith and determination saw her through the school year, setting a precedent for future generations. In later years, Ruby continued her advocacy for education and civil rights by founding the Ruby Bridges Foundation. Her legacy exemplifies how faith and dedication can drive transformative change and inspire others in the ongoing struggle for justice and equality. 60

Lord, as we reflect on Your call to compassion and the example of Ruby Bridges, we ask You to fill us with Your love and mercy. Help us to be kind and generous, showing Your grace in every action. Amen.

Reflective Questions

How can you cultivate an attitude of compassion and mercy in your daily life to reflect God's love in your relationships with others?

....
....
....
....
....
....
....
....
....
....

What aspects of Ruby Bridges' courage and determination inspire you to face challenges and act with compassion in your own life?

....
....
....
....
....
....
....
....

Week 20

Healing through Forgiveness

"Bear with each other and forgive one another if any of you has a grievance against someone. Forgive as the Lord forgave you."
Colossians 3:13

Readings:

Readings:

Day 1: Matthew 6:14
Day 2: Mark 11:25
Day 3: Luke 17:3-4
Day 4: Ephesians 4:31-32
Day 5: Romans 12:17-19
Day 6: 2 Corinthians 2:10
Day 7: Proverbs 19:11

Week's Reflection

This week's theme is "Healing through Forgiveness." Forgiving as God forgives us releases us from the burden of resentment, allowing forgiveness to become a tool for healing and peace in our lives.

Reflections

Day 1: Matthew 6:14 Forgiving others is a pathway to receiving God's forgiveness. By releasing others from their offenses, we too are freed from the weight of resentment.

Day 2: Mark 11:25 Prayer and forgiveness are interconnected; when we forgive others, we make space for God to forgive us and restore our relationships.

Day 3: Luke 17:3-4 Continuous forgiveness reflects God's grace in our lives, teaching us to be persistent in reconciliation and peace, even in the face of repeated offenses.

Day 4: Ephesians 4:31-32 Letting go of bitterness and malice allows kindness and mercy to prevail, reflecting Christ's forgiveness in our daily relationships.

Day 5: Romans 12:17-19 Seeking good and peace in our interactions is an act of faith; leaving revenge to God and practicing forgiveness frees us from unnecessary burdens.

Day 6: 2 Corinthians 2:10 Forgiving others is an act of obedience and faith in Christ, transforming our relationship with God and others, bringing healing and reconciliation.

Day 7: Proverbs 19:11 The wisdom in forgiveness lies in letting go of offenses, demonstrating that self-control and mercy enable us to live in peace and harmony.

Harriet Jacobs

Harriet Jacobs, born in 1813 in Edenton, North Carolina, is a remarkable figure whose life illustrates how faith can drive profound social change. Enduring the harsh conditions of slavery, Jacobs faced relentless exploitation and abuse. Her deep belief in God's justice and her personal faith provided her with the strength to escape and hide in a small attic space for nearly seven years, evading capture and planning her escape to freedom. Her autobiography, Incidents in the Life of a Slave Girl, published in 1861 under the pseudonym Linda Brent, revealed the brutal realities of slavery, especially the sexual exploitation of enslaved women. Jacobs used her writing as a tool to expose these injustices and garner support for the abolitionist movement. Despite immense personal danger, Jacobs remained committed to advocating for freedom and equality. Her steadfast faith and courage not only bolstered the abolitionist cause but also inspired many others to pursue justice and equality. Harriet Jacobs' story is a testament to how faith, resilience, and courage can transform adversity into a powerful force for change. 63

Lord, as we reflect on the healing power of forgiveness and Harriet Jacobs' bravery, we ask for Your guidance to forgive as You have forgiven us, seeking healing and peace in our lives. Amen.

Reflective Questions

How can you apply the principle of forgiveness in conflict situations in your daily life to find healing and peace, as taught in Scripture?

....
....
....
....
....
....
....
....
....
....

What lessons of bravery and resilience can you learn from Harriet Jacobs' life that help you face your own challenges with forgiveness and strength?

....
....
....
....
....
....
....
....

Week 21

Faith in Action

"As the body without the spirit is dead, so faith without deeds is dead."

James 2:26

Readings:

Day 1: Hebrews 11:1
Day 2: James 2:17
Day 3: Galatians 5:6
Day 4: Matthew 7:21
Day 5: Ephesians 2:10
Day 6: 1 John 3:18
Day 7: Romans 12:6

Week's Reflection

This week's theme is "Faith in Action." True faith is not just belief but a force that drives our actions and decisions, manifesting through deeds that reflect God's love and will in our lives.

Reflections

Day 1: Hebrews 11:1 Faith is the foundation of our hope and conviction. While we await what is unseen, we must act in alignment with that faith to make it tangible in our lives.

Day 2: James 2:17 Faith without action is inert. For our faith to be alive, it must manifest in works that demonstrate our trust in God and His purpose for us.

Day 3: Galatians 5:6 Genuine faith is expressed through love and actions. It's not enough to believe; our deeds should be an extension of our faith, reflecting Christ's love in every action.

Day 4: Matthew 7:21 Claiming to know Christ is not enough; our actions must align with His will. True faith is demonstrated by doing the will of God in our daily lives.

Day 5: Ephesians 2:10 God has created us to do good works. Our faith is put into practice through the actions we are called to perform, showcasing His love and justice to the world.

Day 6: 1 John 3:18 Genuine love is expressed not only in words but in concrete actions. Our faith is strengthened and manifested in how we act and live out the truth of God's love.

Day 7: Romans 12:6 Every gift and ability we receive from God should be used in action. Our faith is reflected in how we apply these gifts for His glory and to serve others.

Madam C.J. Walker

Madam C.J. Walker, born Sarah Breedlove on December 23, 1867, in Louisiana, exemplified how faith and perseverance can transform challenges into monumental success. Orphaned young and working as a laundress, Walker's rise to prominence was fueled by her unshakable belief in herself and her faith in God. Confronting scalp ailments of her own, she developed hair care products designed for African American women. Her creation of the "Walker Method" not only addressed a pressing need but also established a thriving business empire. Walker's faith extended beyond her business success. She devoted her resources to philanthropy and social justice, generously supporting educational institutions and civil rights causes. Driven by a belief in uplifting others, she provided employment and training for Black women, helping them gain financial independence and self-worth. Her story is a powerful illustration of how faith in oneself and in a higher purpose can lead to extraordinary achievements and societal impact. Madam C.J. Walker's legacy remains a beacon of hope, demonstrating that faith, determination, and a commitment to justice can inspire transformative change.

Lord, as we reflect on the importance of active faith and the legacy of Madam C.J. Walker, we ask for Your strength to live out our faith through our actions. May our deeds reflect Your love and justice. Amen.

Reflective Questions

How can you integrate the teachings on faith and works into your daily life to ensure that your faith is not just a belief but an active force guiding your actions?

....
....
....
....
....
....
....
....
....

What concrete steps can you take in your life, inspired by Madam C.J. Walker's success and actions, to apply your faith in a way that makes a positive impact on your community?

....
....
....
....
....
....
....
....

Week 22

Peace in God's Presence

"The Lord gives strength to his people; the Lord
blesses his people with peace."
Psalm 29:11

Readings:

Day 1: Isaiah 26:3
Day 2: John 14:27
Day 3: Philippians 4:6-7
Day 4: Psalm 34:14
Day 5: Matthew 11:28
Day 6: Romans 15:13
Day 7: 2 Thessalonians 3:16

Week's Reflection

This week's theme is "Peace in God's Presence." True peace comes from being in God's presence, trusting in His strength, and finding rest in His love, beyond our external circumstances.

Reflections

Day 1: Isaiah 26:3 God promises complete peace when we focus our thoughts on Him. Inner peace flourishes through trust and a constant dedication to His presence.

Day 2: John 14:27 The peace that Jesus offers is not like the world's; it is a deep and lasting calm. In times of anxiety, we can find peace in His presence, allowing His tranquility to soothe our hearts.

Day 3: Philippians 4:6-7 By presenting our concerns to God with gratitude, His peace, which surpasses human understanding, will guard our hearts and minds, easing our deepest anxieties.

Day 4: Psalm 34:14 Seeking and pursuing peace requires turning away from evil and doing good. Peace is found in the conscious action of living according to God's principles.

Day 5: Matthew 11:28 Jesus invites us to rest in Him. Amidst the turmoil and weight of our lives, finding rest in His presence is a promise that brings relief and peace.

Day 6: Romans 15:13 God desires to fill us with joy and peace, increasing our hope through the Holy Spirit. Peace in our lives is a sign of our faith and hope in His power.

Day 7: 2 Thessalonians 3:16 God's peace accompanies us in all aspects of life. By trusting in His presence, we find constant and secure peace amid any challenge.

Mary Prince

Mary Prince was a courageous and influential abolitionist whose life was deeply marked by her unwavering faith in God. Born into slavery in Bermuda, Mary endured the brutalities of servitude but remained resilient, guided by her profound belief in divine providence. In 1828, she published her autobiography, "The History of Mary Prince," a groundbreaking work that shed light on the harrowing experiences of enslaved women. Her narrative not only challenged the injustices of slavery but also reflected her inner strength and hope, rooted in her trust in God. Mary's bravery in speaking out against the oppression she faced was fueled by her faith, which provided her with a sense of peace and purpose. Her legacy continues to inspire Black women, especially those struggling with anxiety, by demonstrating how faith can offer solace and strength amidst adversity. Mary Prince's story is a testament to embracing God's peace and finding courage in the face of profound challenges.

Lord, as we seek peace in Your presence, inspired by Mary Prince's legacy, we ask that You strengthen us and fill us with Your peace. May Your tranquility guide our actions toward justice and love. Amen.

Reflective Questions

How can you cultivate God's peace in your daily life, especially in moments of anxiety, and allow His peace to surpass your worries?

....
....
....
....
....
....
....
....
....
....

How can Mary Prince's unwavering faith and courage inspire you to embrace God's peace and find strength in your journey through anxiety?

....
....
....
....
....
....
....
....
....

Week 23

Hope in God's Promises

"But the Lord is faithful, and he will strengthen you and
protect you from the evil one."
2 Thessalonians 3:3

Readings:

Day 1: Isaiah 41:10
Day 2: Psalm 46:1
Day 3: 1 Peter 5:7
Day 4: Jeremiah 29:11
Day 5: Philippians 4:13
Day 6: Hebrews 10:23
Day 7: Romans 15:13

Week's Reflection

This week, we reflect on "Hope in God's Promises." Just as God promises strength and protection in 2 Thessalonians, we are reminded that His faithfulness upholds us in times of uncertainty and anxiety.

Reflections

Day 1: Isaiah 41:10 God assures us of His constant presence, dispelling fear. His promise of strength is a refuge amid our struggles, reminding us that we are never alone.

Day 2: Psalm 46:1 This Psalm reminds us that God is our refuge and strength. In times of despair, His presence brings us peace and helps us face any adversity.

Day 3: 1 Peter 5:7 This verse invites us to cast our anxieties on God. His promise is that He cares for us and offers relief from our emotional burdens.

Day 4: Jeremiah 29:11 God has plans for our hope. In times of uncertainty, we can trust in His divine plan, knowing He guides us towards a hopeful future.

Day 5: Philippians 4:13 This verse reminds us that with Christ, we have the strength to overcome any challenge. Our hope is based on His power, not our own strength.

Day 6: Hebrews 10:23 God is faithful to His promises. This verse encourages us to hold fast to our hope, knowing that His faithfulness will never fail us.

Day 7: Romans 15:13 The God of hope fills us with joy and peace. This verse reminds us that by trusting in God, we can experience abundant and enduring hope.

Dr. Yvonne C. Johnson

Dr. Yvonne C. Johnson, a distinguished leader in global health and education, achieved remarkable success by integrating her deep faith and commitment to social justice. Born with a passion for addressing inequalities, she pursued a career in medicine and public health, driven by her belief in the transformative power of compassionate service. In 1998, she founded the Global Health and Education Foundation, guided by her faith and vision to provide essential healthcare and educational resources to underserved communities. Her work spans continents, focusing on maternal and child health, disease prevention, and educational empowerment, all rooted in her dedication to making a difference. Dr. Johnson's initiatives offer not only medical care but also the knowledge and tools necessary for individuals to build healthier, more prosperous lives. Her holistic approach combines health and education, reflecting her belief in the power of comprehensive support for sustainable development. Dr. Johnson's faith and perseverance have inspired many, especially women in global health, showing that dedication and compassion can drive profound change. Her legacy highlights how a strong commitment to one's principles can lead to meaningful progress and a more equitable world.

Lord, as we reflect on Your promises of strength and protection, inspire us to keep our hope firmly in You. Just as Dr. Johnson did with her mission, may we trust in Your faithfulness and continue moving forward with faith. Amen.

Reflective Questions

How can you apply God's promises of strength and protection in your daily life to overcome moments of anxiety and difficulty?

....
....
....
....
....
....
....
....
....
....

What lessons can you learn from Dr. Yvonne C. Johnson about maintaining hope and faith amidst challenges, and how can you apply these lessons to your own life?

....
....
....
....
....
....
....
....

Week 24

Strength in God's Word

"I can do all this through him who gives me strength."
Philippians 4:13

Readings:

Day 1: Psalm 119:28
Day 2: Isaiah 40:29
Day 3: 2 Corinthians 12:9
Day 4: Ecclesiastes 4:12
Day 5: Nehemiah 8:10
Day 6: Romans 8:31
Day 7: Ephesians 6:10

Week's Reflection

This week, we focus on "Strength in God's Word." Just as the Apostle Paul relies on the power of Christ to face any situation, we find our strength and ability to overcome challenges through the Word of God.

Reflections

Day 1: Psalm 119:28 When we feel downcast, the Word of God gives us strength. The psalmist shows how Scripture can revive our spirit in times of weakness.

Day 2: Isaiah 40:29 God renews our strength when we are weary. His power transforms our weakness into strength, reminding us that in Him, we find energy and encouragement.

Day 3: 2 Corinthians 12:9 God reveals that His grace is sufficient. In our weaknesses, His power is made more evident, reminding us that His strength is perfected in our frailties.

74

Day 4: Ecclesiastes 4:12 The Word of God teaches us the importance of community and mutual support. With His strength and the backing of others, we are stronger in the face of any challenge.

Day 5: Nehemiah 8:10 The joy of the Lord is our strength. By finding joy in His presence and His promises, we gain the strength to overcome obstacles and stand firm.

Day 6: Romans 8:31 If God is with us, no one can be against us. His Word assures us that His support gives us the courage to face any adversity.

Day 7: Ephesians 6:10 We must strengthen our lives with God's power. By being equipped with His strength, we face trials with confidence, knowing He is our source of power.

Keshia Chanté

Keshia Chanté, a Canadian singer, actress, and mental health advocate, has become a compelling voice in addressing mental health stigma. Born in 1988, Chanté achieved early success as a celebrated artist in the music industry. Yet, her journey was deeply shaped by personal struggles with mental health, leading her to advocate passionately for emotional and psychological well-being. Chanté attributes her resilience and success to her faith, which has guided her through challenges and fueled her advocacy. She uses her platform to highlight the significance of mental health, especially in marginalized communities where stigma can be a major barrier to seeking help. Through her music, public speaking, and social media, Chanté openly shares her experiences, encouraging others to prioritize their mental health and seek support. Her faith and transparency have helped dismantle the barriers surrounding mental illness discussions. Moreover, Chanté's story illustrates how faith and determination can transform adversity into a powerful force for change. By embracing her struggles and advocating for mental health, she has shown that personal trials can be overcome and used as a platform for inspiring and effecting positive change in others' lives.

Lord, as we meditate on Your Word and the example of Keshia Chante, strengthen our spirit and encourage us to face our struggles with courage. May Your power sustain us and propel us to live with hope and faith. Amen.

Reflective Questions

How can you apply the strength offered by God's Word to face anxieties and challenges in your daily life?

....
....
....
....
....
....
....
....
....
....

How can you follow Keshia Chante's example in your own life to transform your personal challenges into opportunities to empower others and promote emotional well-being?

....
....
....
....
....
....
....
....

Week 25

Patience in God's Plan

"Wait for the Lord; be strong and take heart and wait for
the Lord."
Psalm 27:14

Readings:

Day 1: Isaiah 40:31
Day 2: Lamentations 3:25
Day 3: James 5:7-8
Day 4: Romans 8:25
Day 5: Psalm 37:7
Day 6: Proverbs 3:5-6
Day 7: Hebrews 10:36

Week's Reflection

This week, we explore "Patience in God's Plan." As we face challenges and times of waiting, we trust that God has a perfect plan, and our patience in His will will strengthen us.

Reflections

Day 1: Isaiah 40:31 Patience is renewed as we wait on God. Like the wings of eagles, our strength and vigor are restored when we trust in His perfect timing.

Day 2: Lamentations 3:25-26 The Lord is good to those who trust in Him. Waiting patiently for His intervention reminds us that His plan is always for our good.

Day 3: James 5:7-8 The patience of the farmer teaches us to wait with hope and without despair. The coming of the Lord is near, and our patience in His plan is rewarded.

Day 4: Romans 8:25 Waiting patiently is an expression of our faith. Hope in what we do not see strengthens our character and draws us closer to divine purposes.

Day 5: Psalm 37:7 Resting in the Lord helps us remain calm amid uncertainty. Patience is a form of trust that God is working on our behalf.

Day 6: Proverbs 3:5-6 Trusting the Lord with all our heart and not relying on our own understanding guides us on the path of patience and divine wisdom.

Day 7: Hebrews 10:36 Patience is necessary to receive God's promise. Trusting in His plan requires active waiting and perseverance in faith.

Bessie Coleman

Bessie Coleman, born in 1892 in Atlanta, Texas, was a pioneering aviator whose faith and determination propelled her to greatness. Confronting poverty and the dual challenges of racism and sexism, she remained steadfast in her dream of becoming a pilot. With unwavering faith, Coleman saved diligently and traveled to France, where she obtained her pilot's license in 1921 from the Fédération Aéronautique Internationale, making her the first Black woman to achieve this feat. Returning to the U.S., Coleman became a celebrated stunt pilot, showcasing her remarkable skills and daring aerial feats. Her faith and commitment to equality drove her to use her success to challenge racial barriers and inspire other African Americans to enter aviation. She refused to participate in segregated events, standing firm in her belief in justice and inclusion. Though her life ended tragically in a plane crash in 1926, Coleman's legacy endures. Her faith and courage paved the way for future Black aviators and served as a beacon of hope for overcoming adversity and pursuing one's dreams with conviction and resilience.

Lord, as we reflect on the patience Bessie Coleman demonstrated in her quest to soar high and the promises in Your Word, strengthen our spirit to wait on Your plan with hope and courage. Amen.

Reflective Questions

How can you apply the patience taught in Scripture to better handle difficult situations and anxiety in your daily life?

....
....
....
....
....
....
....
....
....
....

How can you follow Bessie Coleman's example in your own life to persevere in your dreams and goals, even when facing significant obstacles?

....
....
....
....
....
....
....
....
....

Week 26

Faith through Trials

"He gives strength to the weary and increases the
power of the weak."
Isaiah 40:29

Readings:

Day 1: 2 Corinthians 12:9
Day 2: Psalm 46:1
Day 3: Hebrews 11:1
Day 4: James 1:2-4
Day 5: Romans 5:3-5
Day 6: 1 Peter 1:6-7
Day 7: Psalm 30:5

Week's Reflection

This week, we focus on "Faith through Trials." In times of weakness and difficulty, God strengthens us and increases our power, teaching us that faith is refined and strengthened through trials.

Reflections

Day 1: 2 Corinthians 12:9 God's grace is sufficient in our weakness. Through our limitations, His power is more clearly manifested, teaching us that in our weakness, we find true strength in Him.

Day 2: Psalm 46:1 God is our refuge and strength in times of trouble. When we face trials, His constant presence offers protection and a firm anchor for our troubled souls.

Day 3: Hebrews 11:1 Faith is the assurance of what we hope for and the conviction of what we do not see. In the midst of trials, this faith drives us to trust in the invisible and the promises of God.

80

Day 4: James 1:2-4 Trials produce perseverance and maturity. Though difficult, challenges are opportunities to grow in our faith and character, making us more complete in Christ.

Day 5: Romans 5:3-5 Suffering produces perseverance, which in turn produces character and hope. This hope, grounded in God's love, will not disappoint us, even when we face difficulties.

Day 6: 1 Peter 1:6-7 Trials refine our faith like gold. Through hardships, our faith is purified and strengthened, demonstrating the genuine value of our trust in God.

Day 7: Psalm 30:5 Weeping may endure for a night, but joy comes in the morning. Though trials may be painful, God transforms suffering into joy and hope through His faithfulness.

Marva Collins

Marva Collins was a pioneering educator who transformed the lives of underprivileged children through her profound faith and determination. Born in Alabama in 1936, Collins encountered significant obstacles, including systemic racism and inadequate resources. In 1975, driven by her deep belief in the potential of every child and guided by her faith, she established the Westside Preparatory School in her Chicago home. Collins' educational philosophy was rooted in her Christian values, emphasizing rigorous instruction and nurturing support. She utilized classical literature and instilled a passion for learning, helping students once deemed "unteachable" to thrive academically and personally. Despite numerous challenges, Collins' school gained acclaim for its remarkable achievements. Her steadfast faith in her students' capabilities and her commitment to quality education inspired many educators and families. Collins' work proved that with love, discipline, and unwavering faith, every child can achieve greatness. Her legacy endures as a powerful testament to how faith and perseverance can transform education, demonstrating that belief in one's mission can lead to extraordinary results. Marva Collins' influence on education highlights the impact of faith-driven dedication and compassion in overcoming adversity.

81

Lord, as we face trials with faith, we remember how Marva Collins overcame barriers with Your strength. Help us to find in our weaknesses the opportunity to experience Your power and grace, trusting that our trials produce a stronger faith. Amen.

Reflective Questions

How can you allow the trials and difficulties in your life to strengthen your faith and draw you closer to God, according to what is taught in Scripture?

....
....
....
....
....
....
....
....
....
....

How can you apply Marva Collins' example of perseverance and faith in your daily life, especially when facing challenges or obstacles?

....
....
....
....
....
....
....
....

Week 27

Joy in God's Presence

"You make known to me the path of life; you will fill me with
joy in your presence."
Psalm 16:11

Readings:

Day 1: Psalm 30:11
Day 2: Isaiah 61:3
Day 3: Philippians 4:4
Day 4: Nehemiah 8:10
Day 5: John 15:11
Day 6: 1 Thessalonians 5:16
Day 7: Psalm 126:3

Week's Reflection

This week, we explore "Joy in the Presence of God." The presence of God transforms our sorrow into joy and guides us toward the fullness of life, revealing the path to lasting and profound joy.

Reflections

Day 1: Psalm 30:11 God turns our mourning into dancing and our sorrow into joy. His presence has the power to transform our tears into gladness, showing us that true comfort comes from His nearness.

Day 2: Isaiah 61:3 The Lord gives us a crown of beauty instead of ashes, the oil of joy instead of mourning. In His presence, we find restoration and deep joy that changes our perspective and renews our spirit.

Day 3: Philippians 4:4 Joy in the Lord is a constant, regardless of our circumstances. By rejoicing in His presence, we discover an unending source of joy that surpasses any difficulty we face.

Day 4: Nehemiah 8:10 The joy of the Lord is our strength. Amid trials and challenges, His joy gives us the strength to move forward, renewing our hope and resilience.

Day 5: John 15:11 Jesus desires for His joy to be in us and for our joy to be complete. His presence fills our lives with a joy that remains unaffected by external circumstances.

Day 6: 1 Thessalonians 5:16-18 We should always rejoice, pray continually, and give thanks in all circumstances. This practice of gratitude and joy in God strengthens our spirit and keeps us connected to His peace.

Day 7: Psalm 126:3 The Lord has done great things for us, and we are filled with joy. Recognizing and thanking God for His blessings fills us with joy and reminds us of His constant faithfulness.

Dorothy Height

Dorothy Height was a trailblazing civil rights and women's rights activist whose achievements were profoundly shaped by her faith. Born in 1912, Height dedicated her life to advancing racial and gender equality in the United States. As president of the National Council of Negro Women (NCNW) for 40 years, her faith was a cornerstone of her leadership, guiding her efforts to uplift African American women and advocate for their rights. Height's unwavering belief in justice and equality drove her involvement in pivotal civil rights events, including the 1963 March on Washington, where she stood with prominent leaders like Martin Luther King Jr. Her faith provided her with resilience and hope amid the prevalent racism and sexism of her era, fueling her dedication to social change. Her ability to inspire others through her commitment and positivity, even in the face of adversity, remains a testament to the transformative power of faith and perseverance. Dorothy Height's legacy underscores the impact of faith-driven activism in creating a more equitable world, and her life's work continues to motivate those striving for justice and equality today.

Lord, as we reflect on Your transformative presence, as Dorothy Height did in her quest for justice, infuse our hearts with Your joy and strength. May Your presence fill our lives with happiness and guide us through any challenges we face. Amen.

Reflective Questions

How can you cultivate an attitude of joy and gratitude in the presence of God, even amidst your current circumstances?

....
....
....
....
....
....
....
....
....

What aspects of Dorothy Height's life and work can you apply to your own journey to face challenges with joy and determination?

....
....
....
....
....
....
....
....

Week 28

Embracing God's Promises

"No matter how many promises God has made, they
are 'Yes' in Christ."

2 Corinthians 1:20

Readings:

Day 1: Hebrews 10:23
Day 2: 2 Peter 1:4
Day 3: Romans 4:21
Day 4: John 14:13-14
Day 5: Psalm 145:13
Day 6: 1 Kings 8:56
Day 7: Isaiah 55:11

Week's Reflection

This week, "Embracing God's Promises," reminds us that all of God's promises are affirmed in Christ. His faithfulness ensures that each promise is true and reliable, providing us with hope and peace.

Reflections

Day 1: Hebrews 10:23 God is faithful to keep His promises. Even in the face of uncertainty, we can fully trust that His word is steadfast and true, and His faithfulness never fails.

Day 2: 2 Peter 1:4 God's promises offer us participation in His divine nature. By embracing them, we are transformed and strengthened, overcoming anxieties with the assurance of His eternal commitment to us.

Day 3: Romans 4:21 Abraham trusted in God's promise, and it was credited to him as righteousness. Our faith in divine promises strengthens us and helps us face our struggles with confidence.

Day 4: John 14:13-14 Jesus promises that our requests made in His name will be answered. In times of anxiety, we can find peace knowing that our prayers are in Christ's hands, who ensures responses.

Day 5: Psalm 145:13 God's kingdom is everlasting, and His promises are faithful. This certainty encourages us to maintain hope and trust in His perfect plan, even when times are tough.

Day 6: 1 Kings 8:56 God has fulfilled every promise made to His people. His faithfulness is a guarantee for our lives, reminding us that He always keeps what He has promised.

Day 7: Isaiah 55:11 Isaiah 55:11 - God's words do not return empty; they always accomplish what they are meant to. We can trust that God's promises will bring fulfillment and transformation into our lives.

Septima Poinsette Clark

Septima Poinsette Clark was a pioneering educator and civil rights activist whose remarkable journey was deeply influenced by her faith in God. Born into a challenging era in Charleston, South Carolina, Clark faced numerous obstacles, but her unwavering trust in divine guidance fueled her determination to effect change. Her dedication to education and empowerment led her to develop crucial literacy programs that played a pivotal role in the civil rights movement, helping countless individuals gain the skills needed to assert their rights and claim their place in society. Clark's commitment to education and equality was not just a career but a calling, driven by a profound sense of purpose and divine assurance. Her work with the Highlander Folk School and the Southern Christian Leadership Conference exemplified her belief in the power of education to transform lives. Septima Poinsette Clark's legacy serves as a powerful reminder of how embracing God's promises can provide strength and clarity in the pursuit of justice and personal growth, inspiring Black women, especially those grappling with anxiety, to find solace and courage in their faith.

Lord, as we reflect on Your faithfulness in every promise, just as Septima Poinsette Clark drew strength from her faith to champion education and civil rights, fill our hearts with peace and hope. Amen.

Reflective Questions

How can you strengthen your trust in God's promises in your daily life, especially when facing challenges and anxieties?

....
....
....
....
....
....
....
....
....
....

How can Septima Poinsette Clark's faith and commitment to justice inspire you to embrace God's promises and find strength in your own journey through anxiety?

....
....
....
....
....
....
....
....

Week 29

Wisdom in God's Guidance

"If any of you lacks wisdom, you should ask God, who gives generously to all without finding fault, and it will be given to you."
James 1:5

Readings:

Day 1: Proverbs 2:6
Day 2: James 1:5
Day 3: Psalm 111:10
Day 4: Isaiah 30:21
Day 5: Ecclesiastes 7:12
Day 6: Job 12:13
Day 7: Colossians 1:9

Week's Reflection

This week, "Wisdom in God's Guidance," reminds us that asking God for wisdom results in His generous and perfect counsel, essential for navigating life and facing anxieties with confidence and divine direction.

Reflections

Day 1: Proverbs 2:6 Wisdom comes from God and is a gift for those who seek it. This assurance guides us in times of uncertainty, reminding us that in Him we find the understanding needed to confront our worries.

Day 2: James 1:5 God promises wisdom without reproach if we ask for it. In moments of anxiety, we can trust in His generosity and seek His guidance to gain clarity and peace in our decisions.

Day 3: Psalm 111:10 The fear of the Lord is the beginning of wisdom. By acknowledging His sovereignty, we find peace and direction, which is vital for reducing anxiety and facing challenges with confidence.

89

Day 4: Isaiah 30:21 God guides us with His wisdom in our daily walk. His direction is clear and reliable, ensuring that even in confusion, we find the right path to peace and security.

Day 5: Ecclesiastes 7:12 Wisdom is a protection, just like money. In times of uncertainty, its power to offer peace and stability becomes a valuable resource that helps us manage anxiety.

Day 6: Job 12:13 God possesses infinite wisdom and power. Recognizing His supremacy encourages us to seek His counsel for answers and to face our concerns with deep understanding.

Day 7: Colossians 1:9 Asking God for wisdom and spiritual understanding is crucial for walking in His will. His guidance provides peace and direction, essential for overcoming anxiety and living with purpose and confidence.

Esther Mahlangu

Esther Mahlangu, born in 1935 in the Mpumalanga province of South Africa, is a celebrated artist whose faith and cultural heritage have profoundly shaped her work. From an early age, she was guided by the spiritual teachings and traditions of her community, which were imparted by the women in her family. Mahlangu's art, marked by bold geometric patterns and vivid colors, is deeply influenced by her faith and connection to Ndebele traditions, which she initially applied to the walls of homes as part of cultural rites. Her commitment to her spiritual beliefs and cultural practices gained international acclaim when she was invited to showcase her work at a 1989 exhibition in Paris. This pivotal moment led to global recognition and collaborations with major brands like BMW, Rolls-Royce, and Belvedere Vodka, extending Ndebele art to an international audience. Mahlangu's faith also drives her role as a cultural ambassador, empowering women and preserving Ndebele heritage. She has dedicated herself to teaching younger generations the art of Ndebele painting, ensuring the continuity of this cherished tradition. Esther Mahlangu's life and achievements illustrate how faith and cultural dedication can transcend boundaries and inspire people worldwide. Her work is a testament to the transformative power of art rooted in deep spiritual and cultural conviction.

Lord, as we seek Your wisdom and guidance, just as Esther Mahlangu did with her art, infuse us with peace and understanding. Guide us with Your wisdom to face our anxieties and live with confidence. Amen.

Reflective Questions

How can you apply divine wisdom to your daily decisions to better manage anxiety and find peace amid challenges?

....
....
....
....
....
....
....
....
....
....

How does Esther Mahlangu's success and commitment to her art inspire you to use your talents and knowledge to face your own anxieties and serve others?

....
....
....
....
....
....
....
....

Week 30

Finding Strength in Adversity

"But he said to me, 'My grace is sufficient for you, for my
power is made perfect in weakness.'"
2 Corinthians 12:9

Readings:

Day 1: 2 Corinthians 12:9
Day 2: Isaiah 40:29
Day 3: Psalm 46:1
Day 4: Philippians 4:13
Day 5: 2 Timothy 1:7
Day 6: Hebrews 4:15-16
Day 7: Romans 8:28

Week's Reflection

This week, "Finding Strength
in Adversity," teaches us that
God's grace upholds us in our
weaknesses, revealing His
perfect power through our
struggles. In times of
difficulty, His strength
becomes our greatest aid.

Reflections

Day 1: 2 Corinthians 12:9 God reminds us that His grace is sufficient, and
His power is displayed in our weaknesses. Embracing this allows us to find
strength amid our struggles and witness His power at work in our lives.

Day 2: Isaiah 40:29 God gives strength to the weary and renews the vigor
of the weak. This promise assures us that in times of exhaustion and
adversity, His support is constant and sufficient to restore and energize
us.

Day 3: Psalm 46:1 God is our refuge and strength, always present in times
of trouble. His constant presence offers us comfort and security,
reminding us that we are not alone in our trials.

Day 4: Philippians 4:13 In Christ, we find the strength to overcome any challenge. This promise encourages us to rely on His power rather than our own limitations, knowing we can face any adversity with His help.

Day 5: 2 Timothy 1:7 God has given us a spirit of power, love, and self-discipline. Facing adversities with this spirit allows us to maintain calm, courage, and mental clarity in difficult times.

Day 6: Hebrews 4:15-16 Jesus understands our weaknesses and invites us to approach Him with confidence. His understanding and mercy offer support in our struggles and help us find grace in times of need.

Day 7: Romans 8:28 God works in all things for the good of those who love Him. This truth assures us that even in our difficulties, His purpose is redemptive, and His plan is directed toward our well-being and growth.

Nannie Helen Burroughs

Nannie Helen Burroughs was an inspiring educator and activist whose life was a testament to finding strength in adversity through her steadfast faith in God. Born into a world fraught with challenges, Burroughs faced systemic racism and limited opportunities, yet her unwavering belief in divine guidance fueled her resolve to make a profound impact. She dedicated her life to education and empowerment, founding the National Training School for Women and Girls in Washington, D.C., which became a beacon of hope and opportunity for countless Black women. Her commitment to education and social justice was driven by a deep sense of purpose and trust in God, which provided her with resilience and courage. Burroughs' efforts to uplift and educate her community reflect her belief that faith can be a source of immense strength during difficult times. Her legacy continues to inspire Black women, particularly those experiencing anxiety, showing that embracing one's faith and purpose can lead to transformative change and personal empowerment. Nannie Helen Burroughs' life serves as a powerful reminder that strength can be found even in the face of the greatest challenges.

Lord, as we face our struggles, grant us the strength that Your grace provides. May we, like Nannie Helen Burroughs, find courage and purpose through Your guidance. Amen.

Reflective Questions

How can you apply the promise that God's grace is sufficient to find strength in your moments of weakness and adversity?

....
....
....
....
....
....
....
....
....
....

How can Nannie Helen Burroughs' faith and resilience inspire you to find strength in adversity and overcome your own challenges?

....
....
....
....
....
....
....
....

Week 31

Trusting God's Timing

"To everything there is a season, and a time for every matter
under heaven."
Ecclesiastes 3:1

Readings:

Day 1: Ecclesiastes 3:1
Day 2: Psalm 27:14
Day 3: Isaiah 40:31
Day 4: 2 Peter 3:8
Day 5: Proverbs 3:5-6
Day 6: Lamentations 3:25
Day 7: Romans 8:28

Week's Reflection

"Trusting God's Timing" teaches us to accept that every event has its appointed time under heaven. In our anxieties, we must trust that God has a perfect plan and divine timing for every aspect of our lives.

Reflections

Day 1: Ecclesiastes 3:1 This verse reminds us that everything has a designated time from God. Embracing this principle helps us find peace in uncertainties, trusting that His plan is perfect and aligned with the right timing.

Day 2: Psalm 27:14 The Psalm encourages us to wait on the Lord with courage. Though waiting can be challenging, trusting in His perfect timing and purpose gives us strength and confidence to face challenges with hope.

Day 3: Isaiah 40:31 God promises to renew our strength as we trust in His timing. Patience during our waits strengthens our faith and allows us to experience His grace and power in times of weakness.

Day 4: 2 Peter 3:8 This verse reminds us that God's timing is not our timing. His patience offers us the chance to grow and prepare to receive His blessings at the perfect moment.

Day 5: Proverbs 3:5-6 Trusting in the Lord rather than our limited understanding guides us through uncertainty. By submitting to His direction, we find peace in the divine timing He has prepared for us.

Day 6: Lamentations 3:25 God is good to those who wait for Him. In times of anxiety and waiting, His goodness sustains us and encourages us to trust that His plan is always the best and in progress.

Day 7: Romans 8:28 God works in all things for the good of those who love Him. This verse assures us that even our difficulties have a purpose under His perfect timing, guiding us towards His ultimate plan.

Henrietta Lacks

Henrietta Lacks (1920-1951) was a remarkable woman whose legacy of courage and resilience continues to inspire. Despite facing the harsh realities of her time, Lacks' unwavering faith in God guided her through profound challenges. Diagnosed with cervical cancer, her cells were unknowingly harvested and became one of the most valuable tools in medical research, leading to countless breakthroughs in science and medicine. Lacks' enduring faith provided her with strength during her illness, and her cells, known as HeLa cells, have contributed to significant advancements in medical science, including the development of vaccines and cancer treatments. Her story exemplifies how trusting in God's timing can bring about transformative outcomes, even amidst adversity. Henrietta Lacks' life and legacy remind Black women, especially those experiencing anxiety, that their strength and faith can lead to extraordinary impacts, even in circumstances beyond their control. Her enduring influence serves as a testament to the power of trusting in a higher purpose and the incredible potential that can emerge from unwavering faith.

Lord, as we trust in Your perfect timing, inspire us with the courage of Henrietta Lacks to wait with hope and act with purpose. May our lives reflect patience and faith in Your divine plan. Amen.

Reflective Questions

How can you apply the teaching of trusting in God's timing to address your anxieties and find peace in your current waits?

....

....

....

....

....

....

....

....

....

....

How can Henrietta Lacks' faith and resilience inspire you to trust in God's timing and find peace amid your own challenges?

....

....

....

....

....

....

....

....

Week 32

Resilience Through Faith

"The righteous cry out, and the Lord hears them; he
delivers them from all their troubles."

Psalm 34:17

Readings:

Day 1: Psalm 34:17

Day 2: Isaiah 43:2

Day 3: 2 Corinthians 4:8-9

Day 4: Romans 5:3-4

Day 5: Philippians 4:13

Day 6: Hebrews 12:1-2

Day 7: 1 Peter 5:10

Week's Reflection

"Resilience Through Faith"
teaches us that even in times
of difficulty, God hears us and
helps us overcome challenges.
Our faith in His power
provides us with the strength
needed to face and surmount
any adversity.

Reflections

Day 1: Psalm 34:17 This verse assures us that God hears our cries and
delivers us from our troubles. Faith in His response and perfect timing is
key to maintaining hope and resilience in difficult times.

Day 2: Isaiah 43:2 God promises to be with us in the toughest trials.
When we go through fire or turbulent waters, His presence guides and
protects us, strengthening our faith and resilience every step of the way.

Day 3: 2 Corinthians 4:8-9 Though we face tribulations and adversities,
we are not defeated. This passage reminds us that through faith, we can
be resilient, enduring hardships without losing hope or faith in God.

98

Day 4: Romans 5:3-4 Suffering produces perseverance, and perseverance produces character. Our faith is strengthened through trials, and each difficulty prepares us for greater strength and a deeper relationship with God.

Day 5: Philippians 4:13 God gives us the strength to face any challenge. With His help, there is no adversity we cannot overcome. This verse encourages us to trust in His power and stand firm in our faith.

Day 6: Hebrews 12:1-2 We run the race of life with perseverance, looking to Jesus as our example. His example of faith and endurance inspires us to move forward, trusting in His support in our own struggles.

Day 7: 1 Peter 5:10 After suffering for a while, God will restore and strengthen us. This verse reminds us that despite difficulties, God has a purpose for our resilience and offers us renewal and strength.

Mahalia Jackson

Mahalia Jackson was an iconic gospel singer whose life exemplified resilience through unwavering faith in God. Born in New Orleans, Jackson overcame numerous obstacles, including poverty and personal hardships, to become a leading figure in gospel music. Her powerful voice and deep spiritual commitment made her a beacon of hope and inspiration, both in her music and her activism. Jackson's faith guided her through trials and propelled her to use her talent for social change, including supporting the Civil Rights Movement. Despite facing many challenges, her belief in divine purpose and guidance sustained her. Jackson's story serves as a profound example of how faith can provide strength and perseverance. For Black women dealing with anxiety, her life offers a testament to the power of resilience through faith. Mahalia Jackson's legacy encourages finding solace and strength in one's spiritual beliefs to overcome adversity and inspire others. Her journey is a powerful reminder that faith can be a source of profound resilience.

Lord, as we seek to be resilient through our faith, teach us to trust in Your power to overcome any adversity. Just as Dr. Bath turned her challenges into triumphs, strengthen our faith and renew our hope. Amen.

Reflective Questions

How can you apply the promise that God hears and delivers those who cry out to Him in your daily life to find strength and resilience in your times of distress?

....
....
....
....
....
....
....
....
....
....

How can Mahalia Jackson's faith and resilience inspire you to find strength and perseverance in your own journey through anxiety?

....
....
....
....
....
....
....
....

Week 33

Faith as a Source of Hope

"May the God of hope fill you with all joy and peace as you trust in him,
so that you may overflow with hope by the power of the Holy Spirit."
Romans 15:13

Readings:

Day 1: Jeremiah 29:11
Day 2: Psalm 39:7
Day 3: Romans 8:24-25
Day 4: Hebrews 11:1
Day 5: 2 Corinthians 1:10
Day 6: Lamentations 3:22
Day 7: 1 Peter 1:3

Week's Reflection

"Faith as a Source of Hope" reminds us that faith in God is an inexhaustible source of hope. By trusting in His promises and power, we can find joy and peace, even amidst our most difficult struggles.

Reflections

Day 1: Jeremiah 29:11 God has plans of prosperity and hope for our lives. Our faith in His guidance and purpose provides a horizon of hope, transforming our worries into trust in His divine plan.

Day 2: Psalm 39:7 Our hope is found in God, not in changing circumstances. This verse reminds us that by trusting in God, our hope remains steadfast and constant, offering us peace amidst uncertainty.

Day 3: Romans 8:24-25 Hope in Christ sustains us, even when answers have not yet arrived. Faith helps us wait with patience and confidence, knowing that God will fulfill His promises in His perfect timing.

Day 4: Hebrews 11:1 Faith is the assurance of what we hope for and the conviction of what we do not see. This verse emphasizes that our hope is based on a solid faith in God and His power, even when the path ahead is not clear.

Day 5: 2 Corinthians 1:10 God has delivered us and will continue to deliver us from all troubles. Our faith in His ability to save us from difficulties fills us with hope, knowing that His power and grace are ever-present.

Day 6: Lamentations 3:22-23 God's faithfulness is the foundation of our hope. His endless mercy and love renew us each day, providing an anchor of hope amidst any storm we may face.

Day 7: 1 Peter 1:3 The resurrection of Christ gives us a living hope. Our faith in His victory over death assures us of eternal hope, transforming our perspective and giving us strength to face any challenge.

Henrietta Mears

Henrietta Mears was a trailblazing Christian educator and leader whose life was profoundly shaped by her steadfast faith in God. Born in Kansas, Mears dedicated herself to teaching and youth ministry, making a lasting impact through her innovative approach to Christian education. As the Director of Christian Education at Hollywood Presbyterian Church, she developed influential programs that transformed the lives of countless young people. Mears' unwavering trust in divine guidance enabled her to overcome challenges and inspire others with her vision and dedication. Her faith was not only a source of personal strength but also a wellspring of hope for those she taught. Henrietta Mears' legacy is a powerful example of how faith can provide a foundation of hope and purpose. For Black women dealing with anxiety, her life story offers a testament to the transformative power of believing in God's promises. Mears' journey underscores how faith can be a source of resilience and inspiration in the pursuit of one's goals and dreams. 102

Lord, as we reflect on Your promise of hope and the stories of faith like that of Henrietta Mears, strengthen our confidence in Your power and guidance. Fill us with joy and peace as we await Your intervention in our lives. Amen.

Reflective Questions

How can you apply the concept of hope based on faith, as illustrated in Romans 15:13, to overcome anxiety and daily difficulties in your life?

....
....
....
....
....
....
....
....
....
....

How can Henrietta Mears' faith and dedication inspire you to find hope and strength in your journey through anxiety?

....
....
....
....
....
....
....
....

Week 34

Embracing God's Provision

"And my God will meet all your needs according to the riches of his glory in Christ Jesus."
Philippians 4:19

Readings:

Day 1: Matthew 6:31-33
Day 2: 2 Corinthians 9:8
Day 3: Psalm 23:1-3
Day 4: Philippians 4:6-7
Day 5: Exodus 16:4
Day 6: 1 Kings 17:14
Day 7: Luke 12:24

Week's Reflection

"Embracing God's Provision" teaches us that God meets all our needs according to His infinite riches. Trusting in His provision frees us from anxiety, granting us peace and security in His constant and abundant care.

Reflections

Day 1: Matthew 6:31-33 Jesus reminds us that by seeking first the Kingdom of God, our needs will be met. This verse emphasizes that by prioritizing our relationship with God, He will provide everything we need, easing our anxiety.

Day 2: 2 Corinthians 9:8 God is able to bless us abundantly, ensuring we have everything we need. This promise assures us that by trusting in His provision, we can face any challenge with a spirit of gratitude and hope.

Day 3: Psalm 23:1-3 The Lord is our Shepherd; we shall not want. This psalm invites us to rest in the certainty that God takes care of us, guiding and providing for our needs, removing our worries.

104

Day 4: Philippians 4:6-7 By presenting our requests to God with thanksgiving, we experience the peace that surpasses all understanding. This verse teaches us that prayer and gratitude are key to trusting in divine provision.

Day 5: Exodus 16:4 God provided manna in the desert for His people. This daily provision reminds us that, even in difficult situations, God will give us what we need at the right time.

Day 6: 1 Kings 17:14 God's provision for the widow at Zarephath demonstrates His ability to meet our needs in times of scarcity. Trusting His promise encourages us to face our shortages with faith and hope.

Day 7: Luke 12:24 God cares for the birds of the air, and how much more for us. This verse reminds us of our worth to God and that He takes care of our needs, inviting us to trust in His generosity.

Serita Jakes

Serita Jakes is a highly esteemed author, speaker, and leader, celebrated for her profound dedication to empowering women through faith. As the wife of Bishop T.D. Jakes, she co-founded The Potter's House Women's Ministry, where her steadfast belief has been crucial in guiding women to navigate life's trials and uncover their true purpose. Raised in Dallas, Texas, Serita encountered substantial personal hardships, including health struggles and loss. Yet, her faith transformed these challenges into powerful avenues for growth and ministry. Her unwavering trust in God has inspired countless women to find strength and resilience in their own lives. In her books, such as The Princess Within and Beside Every Good Man, Serita imparts her wisdom, urging women to recognize their divine worth and embrace their identities as God's daughters. Her conferences and public speaking further amplify her message, creating spaces for women to connect, heal, and flourish. Serita's ministry has profoundly influenced many, illustrating that with faith, empathy, and a spirit of vulnerability, it's possible to overcome adversity and lead a life rich with purpose and joy. Her work stands as a testament to the transformative power of faith and the importance of supporting and uplifting others. 105

Lord, as we meditate on Your promise of provision and the inspiring example of Serita Jakes, help us to embrace Your care and fully trust in Your ability to meet our needs. Fill us with peace and gratitude as we seek Your kingdom. Amen.

Reflective Questions

How can you apply the principle of trusting in God's provision, as shown in Matthew 6:31-33, to reduce anxiety and strengthen your faith in the midst of your daily needs?

....
....
....
....
....
....
....
....
....

How can Serita Jakes' dedication to helping women overcome challenges inspire you to trust in God's provision in your own life and use your experiences to support others?

....
....
....
....
....
....
....
....

Week 35

Strength Through Prayer

"The prayer of a righteous person is powerful and effective."
James 5:16

Readings:

Day 1: 1 Thessalonians 5:16
Day 2: Philippians 4:6
Day 3: Matthew 7:7
Day 4: James 1:5
Day 5: Luke 18:1
Day 6: Romans 8:26
Day 7: 2 Corinthians 12:9

Week's Reflection

"Strength Through Prayer" reveals that the prayer of a righteous person holds immense power. Through constant and sincere prayer, we can find strength and solutions for our anxieties and challenges.

Reflections

Day 1: 1 Thessalonians 5:16-18 Continuous prayer in joy and gratitude connects us with divine power. This verse encourages us to remain in constant communication with God, finding in prayer the strength to face each day.

Day 2: Philippians 4:6 By presenting our requests to God with prayer and thanksgiving, we find peace. This verse shows that prayer is a refuge for our anxieties, offering us tranquility amidst turbulence.

Day 3: Matthew 7:7 Jesus assures us that by seeking sincerely, we will receive answers. Persistent prayer opens the door to divine intervention, providing us the strength to face any difficulty with confidence.

Day 4: James 1:5 God generously offers wisdom when we ask for it. This verse teaches us that prayer is the key to receiving guidance and discernment in times of uncertainty and anxiety.

Day 5: Luke 18:1 Jesus instructs us to pray always and not to lose heart. Constant prayer strengthens and sustains us in times of trial, giving us the resilience to persevere despite difficulties.

Day 6: Romans 8:26 The Holy Spirit intercedes for us in our weakness. This verse assures us that even when we do not know what to ask, prayer is powerful and supported by divine intervention.

Day 7: 2 Corinthians 12:9 God's grace is sufficient and perfected in our weakness. Prayer connects us with God's grace, turning our weaknesses into opportunities to experience His power.

Sojourner Truth

Sojourner Truth was a powerful abolitionist and advocate for women's rights who made a significant impact through her unwavering faith in God. Born into slavery as Isabella Baumfree, she experienced the harsh realities of bondage but found strength in her deep Christian beliefs, which she carried throughout her life and mission. She embarked on a journey as a traveling preacher, renaming herself Sojourner Truth, believing that God had called her to speak the truth about the injustices of slavery and the need for equality. Her speeches were infused with biblical references and a strong conviction that God was on the side of justice. Sojourner's most famous speech, "Ain't I a Woman?" delivered in 1851, showcased her ability to use faith to challenge societal norms and inspire others to fight for equality. Her message resonated with many because of her passionate and authentic delivery, rooted in her personal experiences and her steadfast trust in God's plan. She often spoke of her visions and divine guidance, which she believed gave her the courage to confront the oppressors of her time. Sojourner Truth's legacy demonstrates that through faith and a close relationship with God, one can overcome life's greatest challenges and fight for a world of justice and equality.

Lord, as we meditate on Your promise of power in prayer and the inspiring example of Priscilla Shirer, renew our faith and strengthen our spirit. Through prayer, may we find the strength needed to overcome our anxieties. Amen.

Reflective Questions

How can you integrate a consistent practice of prayer into your daily life to transform moments of anxiety into opportunities to experience God's peace and strength?

....
....
....
....
....
....
....
....
....

How can Priscilla Shirer's testimony about the power of prayer inspire you to face your challenges with greater confidence and seek a deeper connection with God amidst your concerns?

....
....
....
....
....
....
....
....

Week 36

Embracing God's Creativity

"In the beginning God created the heavens and
the earth."
Genesis 1:1

Readings:

Day 1: Psalm 104:24
Day 2: Isaiah 64:8
Day 3: Ephesians 2:10
Day 4: 1 Corinthians 12:4-6
Day 5: Proverbs 3:19
Day 6: Colossians 1:16
Day 7: Hebrews 11:3

Week's Reflection

"Embracing God's Creativity" invites us to recognize and celebrate God's ability to create wonders, and to reflect that creativity in our own lives. His creative power inspires us to be courageous and innovative.

Reflections

Day 1: Psalm 104:24 God has created the world with wisdom and splendor. This verse reminds us that divine creation is vast and intricate, inviting us to appreciate and participate in God's creative act.

Day 2: Isaiah 64:8 Just as the potter shapes the clay, God molds us and gives us purpose. This verse reveals that, despite our fragility, divine creativity shapes and transforms us, giving us a unique purpose.

Day 3: Ephesians 2:10 We are God's workmanship, created for good works. This verse encourages us to embrace our identity as divine creations, using our gifts to make a positive impact in the world.

Day 4: 1 Corinthians 12:4-6 God distributes various gifts and abilities. This passage emphasizes that, within the diversity of talents, we are all part of God's creative design, each contributing to the common good.

Day 5: Proverbs 3:19 God's wisdom founded the earth and established the heavens. This verse reminds us that God's creativity is the foundation of existence, urging us to seek His guidance and wisdom in our creative endeavors.

Day 6: Colossians 1:16 All things were created through Christ and for Him. This passage highlights that creativity and creation find their ultimate purpose in Christ, inviting us to align our own creations with His will.

Day 7: Hebrews 11:3 Faith helps us understand that what is created comes from the unseen. This verse reminds us that divine creativity transforms the intangible into the tangible, calling us to trust in the power of the unseen.

Prathia Hall

Prathia Hall was a pioneering theologian and civil rights leader whose remarkable life was deeply influenced by her steadfast faith in God. Born in Philadelphia, Hall emerged as a passionate advocate for social justice, combining her theological insights with activism to address racial and social inequities. As one of the first Black women to be ordained in the Baptist church, she made significant contributions to the Civil Rights Movement, including her role in the Southern Christian Leadership Conference (SCLC). Hall's sermons and speeches, infused with her belief in divine creativity and purpose, inspired many to engage in the struggle for justice and equality. Her faith provided her with the strength to navigate challenges and envision a world transformed by compassion and creativity. For Black women dealing with anxiety, Prathia Hall's life offers a powerful example of how embracing God's creativity can lead to profound personal and communal growth. Her legacy encourages finding inspiration and resilience through faith to overcome obstacles and foster positive change.

Lord, as we navigate our challenges, fill us with the creativity and strength that only You can provide. May we, like Prathia Hall, use Your divine inspiration to foster growth and positive change. Amen.

Reflective Questions

How can you use the gifts and abilities that God has given you to participate in His creativity and make a difference in the world around you?

....
....
....
....
....
....
....
....
....
....

How can Prathia Hall's embrace of God's creativity inspire you to find new ways to overcome anxiety and foster positive change in your own life?

....
....
....
....
....
....
....
....

Week 37

Trusting God in Transitions

"Commit to the Lord whatever you do, and he will establish your plans."
Proverbs 16:3

Readings:

Day 1: Jeremiah 29:11
Day 2: Proverbs 3:5-6
Day 3: Isaiah 43:19
Day 4: Philippians 4:6-7
Day 5: Psalm 37:5
Day 6: 2 Corinthians 5:7
Day 7: Hebrews 13:8

Week's Reflection

"Trusting God in Transitions" teaches us to rely on God during times of change. By committing our plans to Him, we find stability and direction, even amid uncertainty and transitions.

Reflections

Day 1: Jeremiah 29:11 God has plans for our well-being, even when we face changes. This verse reminds us that His purpose is always for our good, giving us hope in the midst of transitions.

Day 2: Proverbs 3:5-6 Trusting in God rather than our limited understanding guides us in the right direction. In every transition, surrendering our concerns to God allows us to move forward with confidence and security.

Day 3: Isaiah 43:19 God is doing something new in our lives. This verse encourages us to be alert to His work amid change, trusting His ability to make a way in the unexpected.

Day 4: Philippians 4:6-7 Instead of worrying, we should present our requests to God with thanksgiving. His peace, which transcends all understanding, will guard our hearts during transitions.

Day 5: Psalm 37:5 Committing our ways to God ensures that He will direct our steps. This verse invites us to fully trust Him, knowing that His guidance is perfect through any change.

Day 6: 2 Corinthians 5:7 We live by faith, not by sight. During transitions, this passage reminds us to trust in God's guidance even when we cannot clearly see the future.

Day 7: Hebrews 13: 8 Jesus Christ is the same yesterday, today, and forever. This verse assures us that, while our circumstances may change, the constancy of Christ is our steady rock through all transitions.

Iyanla Vanzant

Iyanla Vanzant, a renowned author, spiritual teacher, and life coach, has become a beacon of hope and healing for millions. Born in Brooklyn, New York, she faced a tumultuous childhood marked by poverty, abuse, and instability. These early challenges set the stage for a life filled with personal trials, including a troubled marriage, financial struggles, and the heartbreaking loss of her daughter. Despite these hardships, Iyanla transformed her pain into power by embracing her faith and dedicating herself to the service of others. Her breakthrough came with the publication of Acts of Faith, a daily devotional that resonated with readers seeking spiritual guidance and encouragement. The book's success catapulted her into the spotlight, and she soon became a trusted voice in the self-help movement. Through her television show Iyanla: Fix My Life and numerous workshops, Iyanla has helped countless individuals confront their past traumas and rebuild their lives with purpose and clarity. Her teachings emphasize the importance of self-awareness, forgiveness, and the transformative power of faith. Iyanla Vanzant's journey from adversity to empowerment is a testament to the strength of the human spirit and the profound impact of trusting in divine guidance. 114

Lord, as we navigate the changes and challenges in our lives, strengthen our faith in You. Just as Iyanla Vanzant found strength in her transitions, may we also trust in Your plans and Your peace, guiding us in every moment. Amen.

Reflective Questions

How can you apply the principle of trusting in God during transitions in your life to find peace and direction amidst uncertainty?

....
....
....
....
....
....
....
....
....
....

How does Iyanla Vanzant's experience inspire you to face your own transitions with faith and courage, knowing that God is with you every step of the way?

....
....
....
....
....
....
....
....

Week 38

Embracing the Power of Forgiveness

"For if you forgive other people when they sin against you,
your heavenly Father will also forgive you."
Matthew 6:14

Week's Reflection

"Embracing the Power of Forgiveness" highlights how forgiveness not only heals our relationships but also our soul. By forgiving, we reflect God's grace and release our hearts from the burden of resentment.

Readings:

Day 1: Ephesians 4:32
Day 2: Colossians 3:13
Day 3: Luke 6:37
Day 4: Matthew 18:21-22
Day 5: Psalm 103:12
Day 6: Proverbs 17:9
Day 7: 1 John 1:9

Reflections

Day 1: Ephesians 4:32 True kindness and compassion arise when we forgive others, just as God forgives us. This verse teaches us that forgiveness should be a daily practice, showing genuine love and empathy.

Day 2: Colossians 3:13 Forgiving others as the Lord forgives us is essential for maintaining peace in our lives. This verse encourages us to let go of wounds and embrace forgiveness as a way of life.

Day 3: Luke 6:37 Not judging and forgiving are actions that liberate our spirit. By applying forgiveness, we reflect the character of Christ and open the door to reconciliation and mutual understanding.

Day 4: Matthew 18:21-22 Forgiveness is limitless; we must forgive without counting, as Jesus instructs us. This passage challenges us to practice unconditional forgiveness, freeing ourselves from the burden of revenge and resentment.

Day 5: Psalm 103:12 God has removed our sins from us as far as the east is from the west. This verse reminds us that divine forgiveness is absolute and invites us to emulate this grace in our daily relationships.

Day 6: Proverbs 17:9 Forgiveness fosters peace and restoration in relationships. This verse teaches us that by forgiving, we avoid conflicts and promote an environment of love and reconciliation.

Day 7: 1 John 1:9 Confession and asking for forgiveness bring cleansing and restoration. This verse assures us that by seeking God's forgiveness, we are renewed and empowered to forgive others.

Althea Gibson

Althea Gibson was a trailblazing tennis player whose life was marked by extraordinary courage and unwavering faith in God. Born in Harlem, Gibson rose to prominence in a sport that was predominantly white, breaking racial barriers with her remarkable athleticism and determination. Her faith and resilience were pivotal in overcoming the numerous obstacles she faced in a segregated society. In 1956, she became the first Black player to win a Grand Slam title, achieving this feat again in 1957 and 1958. Gibson's journey was not just about her victories on the court but also her ability to forgive past injustices and focus on her goals. Her strength and grace, coupled with her deep trust in divine guidance, enabled her to inspire future generations of athletes. For Black women dealing with anxiety, Althea Gibson's story underscores the transformative power of embracing forgiveness and letting go of past grievances. Her legacy encourages finding inner peace and strength through faith and resilience.

Lord, as we seek to forgive and find peace, grant us the strength and grace You gave to Althea Gibson. May we, embrace the power of forgiveness and move forward with Your guidance. Amen.

How can you apply the power of forgiveness in your daily life to heal your relationships and heart, drawing from the grace God shows us?

....
....
....
....
....
....
....
....
....
....

How can Althea Gibson's journey of overcoming challenges and embracing forgiveness inspire you to find peace and strength in your own life?

....
....
....
....
....
....
....
....

Week 39

Faith and Perseverance

"Let us not become weary in doing good, for at the proper
time we will reap a harvest if we do not give up."
Galatians 6:9

Readings:

Day 1: Hebrews 12:1-2
Day 2: James 1:2-4
Day 3: Romans 5:3-4
Day 4: Isaiah 40:31
Day 5: 2 Corinthians 4:16
Day 6: Psalm 27:14
Day 7: 1 Peter 5:10

Week's Reflection

"Faith and Perseverance" teaches us to keep our faith strong during challenging times. Just as a farmer waits for the harvest after planting, we must persevere in faith, trusting that God will reward our perseverance in due time.

Reflections

Day 1: Hebrews 12:1-2 Maintaining faith amid trials requires us to focus on Jesus. His example of perseverance inspires us to continue running our race with patience and determination, knowing that He is the source of our strength.

Day 2: James 1:2-4 Life's trials are opportunities to strengthen our faith and character. Through perseverance in difficulties, we develop spiritual maturity that prepares us to reap the benefits of a tested faith.

Day 3: Romans 5:3-4 Trials and difficulties produce endurance, and endurance strengthens our character. By persevering in faith, our character develops, leading us to a firmer and more confident hope in God's promises.

119

Day 4: Isaiah 40:31 Those who wait on the Lord will renew their strength. Faith and patience in the Lord give us the wings to overcome adversity, transforming our weakness into strength and our hope into action.

Day 5: 2 Corinthians 4:16-18 Our momentary troubles are light compared to the eternal glory that awaits us. By persevering in faith, we keep our eyes on the eternal, valuing future blessings over present difficulties.

Day 6: Psalm 27:14 Waiting on the Lord with courage and patience gives us the strength to face any adversity. This verse encourages us to trust in God and wait with faith, knowing that He will fulfill His promises.

Day 7: 1 Peter 5:10 God will use our trials to perfect, establish, and strengthen us. By persevering in faith, we trust that He will restore us and make us steadfast amid our struggles.

Constance Baker Motley

Constance Baker Motley was a pioneering civil rights lawyer and the first Black woman appointed as a federal judge in the United States. Born in 1921 in Harlem, New York, Motley's journey was marked by resilience and an unwavering faith in her mission for justice. After facing racial and gender barriers throughout her education, her faith in her purpose and divine guidance helped her become the first Black woman to graduate from Columbia Law School. Motley's legal career was distinguished by her work with the NAACP Legal Defense Fund, where she collaborated with Thurgood Marshall. Her deep faith provided her with the strength to play a significant role in numerous landmark civil rights cases, including the historic Brown v. Board of Education decision that led to the desegregation of public schools across America. As a lawyer, she argued and won nine out of ten cases before the U.S. Supreme Court, reflecting her belief that her work was guided by a higher purpose. In 1966, Motley broke another barrier by becoming the first Black woman to serve as a federal judge, appointed by President Lyndon B. Johnson. Her faith and dedication to equality had a profound impact on the civil rights movement and continue to inspire those who fight for justice and equal rights today.

120

Lord, as we reflect on the power of faith and perseverance, help us to remain steadfast in our struggles and trust that, just as Constance Baker Motley persevered in her fight for justice, You will reward our faith and efforts. Amen.

How can you apply the principles of perseverance and faith to your current challenges, and what changes can you make to remain steadfast in hope and in God's promises?

....
....
....
....
....
....
....
....
....

How does Constance Baker Motley's example of perseverance and bravery inspire you to face your own challenges and maintain faith in your efforts for justice and change?

....
....
....
....
....
....
....
....

Week 40

Overcoming Obstacles with Faith

"The Lord is my strength and my defense; he has
become my salvation."
Exodus 15:2

Readings:

Day 1: Isaiah 40:29
Day 2: Psalm 18:32
Day 3: Philippians 4:13
Day 4: 2 Corinthians 12:10
Day 5: Hebrews 12:1-2
Day 6: Nehemiah 8:10
Day 7: Romans 8:37

Week's Reflection

This theme highlights how faith in God empowers us to overcome obstacles. Just as the Israelites trusted God to cross the Red Sea, we too can find strength in Him to face our challenges.

Reflections

Day 1: Isaiah 40:29 God provides us with strength when we are exhausted, transforming our weakness into power. His intervention allows us to face challenges with renewed energy.

Day 2: Psalm 18:32 God is our strength in times of uncertainty. His protection ensures our path, giving us confidence to face any obstacle.

Day 3: Philippians 4:13 With God as our source of strength, we are able to overcome any challenge. Our capability comes not from ourselves but from His power.

Day 4: 2 Corinthians 12:10 Recognizing our weaknesses brings us closer to Christ's strength. In our vulnerability, we discover the true divine power to persevere.

Day 5: Hebrews 12:1-2 Perseverance is crucial in our journey of faith. By keeping our eyes on Jesus, the source of our strength, we overcome trials with determination.

Day 6: Nehemiah 8:10 Joy in the Lord is an inexhaustible source of strength. Despite difficulties, His joy propels us and empowers us to move forward.

Day 7: Romans 8:37 In Christ, we are more than conquerors. His love and power enable us to overcome any challenge, reaffirming our victory through His grace.

Janetta B. Cole

Janetta B. Cole is a distinguished educator and public health advocate who has made a significant impact in both academia and community health through her profound faith. Born in 1944, Cole's life has been marked by a deep commitment to advancing opportunities for African American women and improving health outcomes in underserved communities. Her faith guided her groundbreaking achievement as the first Black woman to serve as president of Spelman College, where her leadership, inspired by her spiritual beliefs, transformed the institution into a premier center of excellence for Black women in higher education. Under Cole's guidance, Spelman College gained national recognition for its academic rigor and commitment to the empowerment of young Black women, reflecting her faith-driven dedication to uplifting others. Beyond education, Cole's work extended into public health, where she played a crucial role in developing programs aimed at improving the health and well-being of marginalized populations. Her dedication to social justice and education, fueled by her faith, has left a lasting legacy, influencing countless lives through her advocacy and leadership. Cole's life story is one of resilience and faith, demonstrating that with divine guidance and a passion for justice, it is possible to overcome barriers and inspire others to strive for a better future. Her legacy continues to inspire new generations to pursue education and equality with determination and faith.

Lord, as we reflect on Your strength and the example of Janetta B. Cole, strengthen our faith to face any obstacle with confidence and perseverance. May Your power guide and empower us each day. Amen.

Reflective Questions

How has faith in God helped you face personal obstacles, and which aspects of the Scriptures have provided you with the greatest strength during times of weakness?

....
....
....
....
....
....
....
....
....

How does Janetta B. Cole's life and work inspire you to overcome your own challenges, and what lessons of perseverance and faith can you apply to your daily life?

....
....
....
....
....
....
....
....

Week 41

Embracing New Beginnings

"See, I am doing a new thing! Now it springs up; do you not
perceive it?"
Isaiah 43:19

Week's Reflection

This week's theme encourages
us to embrace new beginnings
with faith. As God promises to
renew and transform our lives,
we must leave behind the old
and trust in the new
opportunities He offers.

Reflections

Day 1: 2 Corinthians 5:17 Accepting Christ renews us. Faith in Him
transforms us, allowing us to leave the past behind and embrace a new
identity in Him.

Day 2: Philippians 3:13-14 Letting go of the past is essential to moving
forward towards what God has in store for us. Perseverance and focus
on the future lead us to the promised blessings.

Day 3: Isaiah 43:18 The past should not define or limit us. God calls us
to look forward, trusting in His plan for our lives and the new
opportunities He brings.

Day 4: Lamentations 3:22-23 Each day brings a new opportunity to experience God's faithfulness. His love and compassion are renewed daily, offering us hope and strength.

Day 5: 1 Peter 5:10 God promises to restore us after difficult times. Faith and perseverance lead us to a new strength and steadfastness in Christ.

Day 6: Psalm 40:3 Our testimony and worship can inspire others. By singing a new song, we reflect the renewal God works in our lives.

Day 7: Revelation 21:5 God is in the process of making everything new. His promise of renewal is firm and true, ensuring that every aspect of our lives can be transformed.

Shirley Ann Caesar

Shirley Ann Caesar, born in 1938, is a renowned gospel singer whose remarkable career reflects profound courage and unwavering faith. Growing up in North Carolina, Caesar's journey from a modest upbringing to becoming a celebrated artist was guided by her steadfast belief in God. Her musical career, spanning over six decades, is marked by numerous awards and a deep impact on gospel music. Caesar's powerful voice and heartfelt lyrics have inspired countless individuals, showcasing how faith can fuel perseverance and creativity. Through periods of personal and professional challenges, her trust in divine guidance helped her embrace new beginnings and continue evolving as an artist. For Black women facing anxiety, Shirley Ann Caesar's story is a testament to the strength found in faith and the ability to start anew. Her life encourages finding hope and renewal through trusting in one's purpose and embracing the opportunities that arise from resilience and divine support.

Lord, as we embrace new beginnings, fill us with the strength and faith that guided Shirley Ann Caesar. May we, like her, find hope and renewal through Your divine support. Amen.

Reflective Questions

How can you apply the promise of renewal that God offers in your daily life to overcome challenges and embrace new beginnings?

....
....
....
....
....
....
....
....
....
....

How can Shirley Ann Caesar's journey of embracing new beginnings inspire you to find strength and renewal in your own life?

....
....
....
....
....
....
....
....

Week 42

Navigating Change with Faith

"Jesus Christ is the same yesterday and today and forever."
Hebrews 13:8

Readings:

Day 1: Malachi 3:6
Day 2: James 1:17
Day 3: Isaiah 41:10
Day 4: Hebrews 12:2
Day 5: Romans 8:28
Day 6: Psalm 102:27
Day 7: 2 Corinthians 1:20

Week's Reflection

This theme highlights the constancy of Christ amidst change. As we face transformations in our lives, our faith in an unchanging God provides us with security and hope to navigate those changes with confidence.

Reflections

Day 1: Malachi 3:6 God's unchanging nature ensures our stability. Despite the changes in life, His faithfulness remains constant, guaranteeing that His love and promises do not waver.

Day 2: James 1:17 God is the source of all blessings, and His immutable nature ensures that all good and perfect gifts come from Him, unaffected by circumstances.

Day 3: Isaiah 41:10 God promises His constant presence and strength, regardless of changing circumstances. His support helps us face any change with courage.

Day 4: Hebrews 12:2 Focusing on Jesus, who remained steadfast through suffering, inspires us to maintain our faith amidst our own trials and changes.

Day 5: Romans 8:28 God works in all things for our good. His plan is constant and eternal, helping us to view changes as part of His purpose for our lives.

Day 6: Psalm 102:27 Despite the fluctuations in our lives, God remains unchanging. His character and promises are steadfast, providing us with security and peace.

Day 7: 2 Corinthians 1:20 All of God's promises are fulfilled in Christ. His steadfastness gives us confidence that His word is reliable and His promises will come to pass.

Valerie Jarrett

Valerie Jarrett, born in 1956, is a prominent figure in American politics and social activism whose achievements have been deeply influenced by her faith. Her influence extends across multiple sectors, including government, business, and philanthropy. Jarrett's career began in Chicago, where she broke barriers as the first African American woman to serve as president of the Chicago Transit Authority. Her faith provided her with the strength to navigate complex challenges and implement effective solutions during this pivotal role. Later, as a senior advisor to President Barack Obama, Jarrett's deep commitment to social justice, economic opportunity, and women's rights was guided by her spiritual beliefs. Her faith helped her address anxiety and difficulties, allowing her to shape domestic policy with resilience and clarity. Jarrett also chaired The Chicago Foundation for Women, further demonstrating her dedication to empowering women and promoting gender equality. Her approach to leadership, marked by resilience, adaptability, and a commitment to justice, reflects how faith and perseverance can drive meaningful change. Jarrett's ability to face adversity with grace and determination serves as a powerful example of how spiritual strength and steadfastness can inspire and influence others. Her legacy continues to encourage women to advocate for their rights and pursue leadership roles in their communities and beyond.

Lord, as we navigate the changes in our lives, help us trust in Your constant presence and the unchanging promises of Your Word. Like Valerie Jarrett, may we face each transition with faith and strength in You. Amen.

Reflective Questions

How can you apply the constancy of Christ in your life to face changes with renewed faith and confidence in His promises?

....
....
....
....
....
....
....
....
....
....

How does Valerie Jarrett's journey inspire you to handle changes and challenges in your personal or professional life with determination and faith in your abilities?

....
....
....
....
....
....
....
....

Week 43

Embracing God's Peace

"And the peace of God, which transcends all understanding, will guard your hearts and your minds in Christ Jesus."
Philippians 4:7

Readings:

Day 1: Psalm 29:11
Day 2: John 14:27
Day 3: Isaiah 26:3
Day 4: 2 Thessalonians 3:16
Day 5: Psalm 34:14
Day 6: Romans 15:13
Day 7: Proverbs 3:24

Week's Reflection

This week focuses on the divine peace that surpasses our understanding. In times of anxiety and chaos, God's peace protects and calms our worries, offering a tranquility that only He can provide.

Reflections

Day 1: Psalm 29:11 God strengthens us and blesses us with peace. His peace, which surpasses any difficulty, sustains us amid life's storms.

Day 2: John 14:27 Christ's peace is different from worldly peace. He invites us to trust His promise and free ourselves from fears, finding security in His presence.

Day 3: Isaiah 26:3 Perfect peace comes from a mind focused on God. Our trust in Him ensures a constant peace, even in uncertain times.

131

Day 4: 2 Thessalonians 3:16 As the Lord of peace, God grants us tranquility in every circumstance. His peace is available at all times and in every situation.

Day 5: Psalm 34:14 Seeking and pursuing peace is a call to live in harmony and goodness, turning away from evil and cultivating peace in our actions.

Day 6: Romans 15:13 God fills us with joy and peace as we trust in Him. His peace empowers us with hope and allows us to experience the power of the Holy Spirit.

Day 7: Proverbs 3:24 The peace God offers transforms our rest, removing fear and ensuring sweet, restorative sleep. His peace wraps us in security.

Miriam Makeba

Miriam Makeba, born in 1932, was a legendary South African singer and civil rights activist whose life exemplified courage and unwavering faith. Known as "Mama Africa," Makeba used her powerful voice and international platform to advocate against apartheid and promote peace. Her music, deeply rooted in traditional African rhythms, carried messages of hope and resistance, resonating with people worldwide. Despite facing immense personal and political challenges, Makeba's faith in God provided her with strength and resilience. Her ability to remain steadfast in her mission, even when exiled from her homeland, reflects a profound inner peace derived from her belief. Makeba's legacy as an artist and activist serves as an inspiring example for Black women facing anxiety, demonstrating how faith can be a source of comfort and motivation. Her story encourages embracing God's peace as a foundation for personal empowerment and societal change.

Lord, as we seek Your peace in our lives, grant us the strength and courage that Miriam Makeba found through her faith. May we, like her, embrace Your peace to empower and inspire our journey. Amen.

Reflective Questions

How can you allow God's peace to transform your daily anxiety, and how can you stay focused on His tranquility during times of unrest?

....
....
....
....
....
....
....
....
....

How can you, like Miriam Makeba, embrace God's peace to find strength in challenging times and use that inner calm to inspire positive change in your life and community?

....
....
....
....
....
....
....
....

Week 44

Finding Courage in Faith

"So do not fear, for I am with you; do not be dismayed, for I am your God. I will strengthen you and help you; I will uphold you with my righteous right hand."
Isaiah 41:10

Readings:

Day 1: Joshua 1:9
Day 2: Psalm 27:1
Day 3: 2 Corinthians 12:9
Day 4: Romans 8:31
Day 5: Isaiah 43:2
Day 6: 1 Peter 5:7
Day 7: Hebrews 13:6

Week's Reflection

This week invites us to find courage through our faith in God. His constant presence and strength enable us to face and overcome our anxieties and fears, trusting in His unconditional support.

Reflections

Day 1: Joshua 1:9 God commands us to be brave and strong, reminding us that His constant presence dispels fear. In any challenge, His guidance is the source of our courage.

Day 2: Psalm 27:1 Trusting in God eliminates fear. By recognizing God as our light and stronghold, we can confront any adversity with courage and without fear.

Day 3: 2 Corinthians 12:9 God's grace is revealed in our weaknesses. By accepting our limitations, we allow His power to strengthen and guide us through difficult times.

Day 4: Romans 8:31 The certainty that God is on our side gives us courage. If God is with us, no challenge is too great to face with confidence and hope.

Day 5: Isaiah 43:2 God promises protection in trials. His presence ensures that we will not be overwhelmed by difficulties, whether by water or fire, He will sustain and protect us.

Day 6: 1 Peter 5:7 Casting our anxieties on God relieves us of emotional burdens. His care provides the peace we need to face our concerns with serenity.

Day 7: Hebrews 13:6 Our confidence in the Lord allows us to live without fear. With God as our support, nothing and no one can threaten our peace or security.

Mary Church Terrel

Mary Church Terrell (1863-1954) was a trailblazing figure in the struggle for civil rights and women's suffrage, whose unwavering faith played a crucial role in her remarkable achievements. Born to formerly enslaved parents, she became one of the first African American women to earn a college degree, demonstrating an extraordinary commitment to education and equality. Her profound faith in God guided her through a life dedicated to activism and advocacy. As a co-founder of the National Association of Colored Women, she championed the cause of civil rights and women's empowerment with a passionate resolve. Terrell's courage was exemplified in her tireless efforts to combat racial and gender discrimination, using her voice and influence to demand justice. Her faith was not just a personal comfort but a source of strength that fueled her activism and resilience. Mary Church Terrell's legacy is a powerful testament to how faith can empower individuals to confront adversity and drive significant social change. Her life continues to inspire those who seek courage in their own journeys, reminding us of the transformative power of faith.

Lord, as we seek Your courage amid our anxieties, strengthen our faith and trust in Your presence. Just as Dr. Black has faced challenges with bravery, help us overcome our fears with Your constant support. Amen.

Reflective Questions

How can you apply God's promises of courage and strength in your daily life to face your fears and anxieties with greater confidence?

....
....
....
....
....
....
....
....
....
....

How can you, like Mary Church Terrell, find courage in your faith to overcome challenges and inspire positive change in your life and community?

....
....
....
....
....
....
....
....

Week 45

Walking in God's Light

"The Lord is my light and my salvation—whom shall I fear?"
Psalm 27:1

Readings:

Day 1: Psalm 119:105
Day 2: John 8:12
Day 3: Isaiah 60:1
Day 4: 2 Corinthians 4:6
Day 5: Ephesians 5:8
Day 6: Matthew 5:14
Day 7: 1 John 1:5

Week's Reflection

This week, we explore how God's light illuminates our path and dispels the darkness of fear and anxiety. Following His light guides and strengthens us, transforming our lives with hope and clarity.

Reflections

Day 1: Psalm 119:105 God's Word lights our path amidst darkness. It provides direction and clarity, guiding us away from uncertainty with His divine light.

Day 2: John 8:12 Following Jesus means walking in His light and living without fear. His presence dispels the shadows of our lives, offering peace and purpose with each step.

Day 3: Isaiah 60:1 God calls us to shine with His light. His glory manifests in us, empowering us to overcome darkness and reflect His hope to a needy world.

Day 4: 2 Corinthians 4:6 God has ignited His light in our hearts, revealing His glory through Christ. This light guides us and fills us with the knowledge and peace of His presence.

Day 5: Ephesians 5:8 Our identity as children of light calls us to live according to God's values. We are called to reflect His light through our daily actions and words.

Day 6: Matthew 5:14 As bearers of Christ's light, we are a beacon of hope. Our presence illuminates the world, showing the love and truth of God to those around us.

Day 7: 1 John 1:5 God is the pure source of light, without any shadow of darkness. In His light, we find the truth and clarity we need to live with confidence and peace.

Alberta Williams King

Alberta Williams King, a revered figure in American civil rights history, exemplified unwavering courage and faith throughout her life. As the mother of Dr. Martin Luther King Jr., she played a vital role in shaping the values that drove the civil rights movement. Despite the tremendous personal and societal challenges she faced, Alberta's steadfast belief in God provided her with immense strength and resolve. Her commitment to her faith was evident in her work as a dedicated educator and church organist, where she used her position to uplift and inspire her community. Alberta's influence extended far beyond her immediate surroundings, as her values and dedication to justice contributed significantly to the broader fight for civil rights. Her legacy of resilience, driven by her deep faith, continues to inspire countless individuals. In times of adversity, Alberta Williams King's life serves as a beacon of hope, demonstrating how trust in God's guidance can empower one to walk in light and lead others towards positive change.

Lord, as we strive to walk in Your light, let us draw strength from the faith that guided Alberta Williams King. May we, like her, find courage in Your presence to lead with purpose and inspire positive change. Amen.

Reflective Questions

How can you apply God's light in your daily life to face your fears and anxieties, and how does it help you live with a renewed perspective of hope and clarity?

....
....
....
....
....
....
....
....
....

How can you, like Alberta Williams King, embrace your faith to find strength and guidance in your journey, and how can this inspire you to make a positive impact in your community?

....
....
....
....
....
....
....
....

Week 46

God's Faithfulness in Trials

"No temptation has overtaken you except what is common to mankind. And God is faithful; he will not let you be tempted beyond what you can bear."
1 Corinthians 10:13

Readings:

Day 1: Psalm 34:19
Day 2: Isaiah 43:2
Day 3: 2 Timothy 4:17
Day 4: 1 Peter 1:6-7
Day 5: Hebrews 10:23
Day 6: Romans 8:28
Day 7: 2 Corinthians 1:10

Week's Reflection

God is faithful in all our trials. Even when we face challenges, He will not allow them to overwhelm us. His faithfulness strengthens us and assures us that through difficulties, we always find His help and purpose.

Reflections

Day 1: Psalm 34:19 Even amid our troubles, God delivers us. His promises of salvation and support are steadfast, reminding us that we are never alone in our struggles.

Day 2: Isaiah 43:2 God is with us in every challenge, whether it's water, fire, or any trial. His presence protects and sustains us, ensuring that we will not be destroyed by our difficulties.

Day 3: 2 Timothy 4:17 Despite adversities, the Lord gives us the strength to fulfill His purpose. His constant support enables us to overcome trials and proclaim His message of hope.

Day 4: 1 Peter 1:6-7 Trials refine our faith, making it more valuable than gold. Though we may suffer temporarily, these challenges reveal the authenticity of our faith and bring glory to Christ.

Day 5: Hebrews 10:23 We can trust in God's faithfulness. Holding firm to our hope reflects His unbreakable promise and His constant presence in our lives.

Day 6: Romans 8:28 God uses all things for the good of those who love Him. Even our difficulties are part of His plan, transforming our challenges into opportunities for His glory.

Day 7: 2 Corinthians 1:10 God has been faithful in the past and will continue to be in the future. Our hope is in His ongoing power to deliver and guide us through any trial.

Pauli Murray

Pauli Murray was a pioneering figure whose life exemplifies courage and resilience in the face of adversity. An esteemed civil rights activist, lawyer, and scholar, Murray's journey was profoundly influenced by her steadfast faith and belief in divine support. Despite encountering significant challenges, including racial and gender discrimination, she remained unwavering in her commitment to justice and equality. Her faith provided her with the strength to overcome obstacles and advocate for change. Murray's groundbreaking work, including her role in co-founding the National Organization for Women (NOW) and her contributions to legal strategies that influenced landmark civil rights cases, showcases her remarkable ability to turn trials into triumphs. Her unwavering belief in God's guidance and support fueled her determination to create a more just society. Pauli Murray's legacy is a testament to the power of faith in guiding one through trials and achieving profound impact. As we reflect on her story, let us embrace the notion of divine faithfulness and draw inspiration from her example of resilience and commitment.

Lord, as we navigate our own trials, help us find strength in Your faithfulness, just as Pauli Murray did. May her example of perseverance through adversity inspire us to trust in Your guidance and remain steadfast in our journey. Amen.

Reflective Questions

How can you experience and trust in God's faithfulness during your most challenging moments, and how can His promises shift your perspective on your trials?

....
....
....
....
....
....
....
....
....

How can you, like Pauli Murray, find strength in your faith during challenging times and use that resilience to create positive change in your own life?

....
....
....
....
....
....
....
....

Week 47

God's Guidance in Uncertainty

"In all your ways submit to him, and he will make your paths straight."
Proverbs 3:6

Readings:

Day 1: Psalm 32:8
Day 2: Proverbs 16:9
Day 3: Isaiah 30:21
Day 4: James 1:5
Day 5: Psalm 119:105
Day 6: Jeremiah 29:11
Day 7: Proverbs 3:5-6

Week's Reflection

God guides our steps in times of uncertainty. By submitting to His will and trusting in His direction, we find clarity and purpose amid confusion, ensuring that our paths are straight and our hearts are at peace.

Reflections

Day 1: Psalm 32:8 God offers us direction and wisdom with His constant love. In moments of doubt, His guidance is precise and loving, leading us to the right path with His perfect vision.

Day 2: Proverbs 16:9 While we may plan our path, it is God who directs it. Our trust in His plans ensures that our steps are firm and our journey secure.

Day 3: Isaiah 30:21 God promises clear guidance in every decision. His voice leads us at every turn, providing security and certainty amidst uncertainty.

Day 4: James 1:5 Divine wisdom is available to all. By seeking God, we receive the discernment needed to face challenges and make wise decisions.

Day 5: Psalm 119:105 God's word illuminates our path, providing clarity and direction at every step. His guidance keeps us on the path of righteousness and peace.

Day 6: Jeremiah 29:11 God has plans for our well-being, even when we don't understand the immediate purpose. His vision is one of hope and prosperity, ensuring a bright future.

Day 7: Proverbs 3:5-6 Trusting fully in God guides us to righteousness. By submitting to His will, we find stability and direction, easing anxiety about the future.

Marian Wright Edelman

Marian Wright Edelman is a beacon of courage and faith, known for her profound impact on child advocacy and civil rights. From her early days as a lawyer fighting for justice to founding the Children's Defense Fund (CDF), her unwavering faith and trust in God were central to her mission. Edelman dedicated her life to ensuring that all children, regardless of their background, had access to opportunities and protection. Her deep commitment to these values, driven by a belief in divine guidance, empowered her to navigate immense challenges and create substantial changes in legislation and societal attitudes. Through her work, Edelman highlighted the importance of faith as a guiding force in the face of adversity, showing how reliance on spiritual principles can lead to transformative action. Her legacy serves as an inspiring example of how faith can provide clarity and purpose amidst uncertainty, urging us all to seek divine guidance in our own journeys.

Lord, as we face our own uncertainties, may we find inspiration in Marian Wright Edelman's steadfast faith and commitment. Help us to trust in Your guidance as she did, finding clarity and purpose in the midst of challenges. Amen.

Reflective Questions

How can you apply divine guidance in your daily life to face uncertainty and make important decisions with confidence and peace?

....
....
....
....
....
....
....
....
....
....

How can you, like Marian Wright Edelman, find strength in divine guidance to overcome personal uncertainties and inspire growth in your own life?

....
....
....
....
....
....
....
....

Week 48

God's Comfort in Loss

"Blessed are those who mourn, for they will be comforted."
Matthew 5:4

Week's Reflection

God offers comfort in times of loss and pain, drawing near to broken hearts and providing peace that surpasses human understanding. Amidst grief, His love and care strengthen and restore us.

Reflections

Day 1: Psalm 34:18 God draws close to those who are suffering, offering comfort and healing. His nearness in pain transforms our suffering into hope and strength.

Day 2: Isaiah 61:1 God sends His Son to heal broken hearts and set captives free. His mission is to restore and bring release to those facing darkness.

Day 3: 2 Corinthians 1:3-4 The comfort we receive from God enables us to comfort others. His compassion and support allow us to be sources of hope in times of difficulty.

Day 4: John 14:27 Jesus offers us enduring peace that is not found in the world. In the midst of pain, His peace guards our hearts and eases our fears.

Day 5: Psalm 147:3 God heals emotional and physical wounds, providing care and restoration. His love is a constant source of healing in our grieving process.

Day 6: Romans 8:28 God works in all circumstances for our good. Even in the face of loss, His purpose is one of hope and redemption, transforming our pain into purpose.

Day 7: 1 Peter 5:7 We cast our anxieties on God because He deeply cares for us. His love and care provide a safe refuge in times of distress.

Chaka Khan

Chaka Khan, often hailed as the "Queen of Funk," is a legendary singer and philanthropist renowned for her dynamic voice and influential music career. Rising to fame in the 1970s with the band Rufus and her subsequent solo work, Khan became a defining figure in funk, soul, and R&B music. Her powerful voice and hits like "I'm Every Woman" and "Ain't Nobody" cemented her status as an icon. Despite her success, Khan faced personal struggles, including the loss of loved ones and health challenges. Her faith played a crucial role in managing anxiety and maintaining her resolve during these difficult times. Instead of being deterred, her spiritual beliefs fueled her resilience and commitment to making a difference. Beyond her music, Khan is deeply involved in philanthropy, focusing on mental health awareness and youth support. She established the Chaka Khan Foundation to address issues such as homelessness, youth programs, and healthcare access. Khan's journey illustrates how faith and personal trials can be channeled into positive change. Her ability to turn her experiences into advocacy and support for others exemplifies the power of resilience and dedication. Her legacy continues to inspire and uplift, demonstrating that strength, compassion, and faith can transform lives.

Lord, in the midst of pain and loss, we trust in Your comfort and peace. Just as Chaka Khan has found strength and purpose through her struggles, allow us to feel Your nearness and restoration in our own trials. Amen.

Reflective Questions

How can you experience and share the comfort God offers in your daily life, especially when facing losses or emotional challenges?

....
....
....
....
....
....
....
....
....

How can Chaka Khan's resilience and commitment to philanthropy inspire you to find purpose and strength amidst your own losses and difficulties?

....
....
....
....
....
....
....

Week 49

Finding Peace in God's Plan

"You will keep in perfect peace those whose minds are
steadfast, because they trust in you."
Isaiah 26:3

Week's Reflection

Finding peace in God's plan involves fully trusting His direction and promises. By submitting to His will, we receive perfect peace that calms our anxiety and guides us through uncertain times.

Reflections

Day 1: Jeremiah 29:11 God has a plan for each life, filled with hope and prosperity. Trusting in His plan helps us find peace even when the path seems uncertain.

Day 2: Philippians 4:6-7 By presenting our concerns to God with prayer and gratitude, His peace, which surpasses human understanding, protects our hearts and minds.

Day 3: Proverbs 3:5-6 Total trust in God and submission of our paths to Him ensure that He guides our decisions and provides clear direction.

Day 4: Psalm 29:11 God strengthens His people and grants them peace. In His strength, we find the tranquility needed to face any challenge.

Day 5: Matthew 6:34 We should not worry about the future, but trust that each day brings enough grace to handle its difficulties.

Day 6: Romans 15:13 God, the source of hope, fills us with joy and peace as we trust in Him, allowing us to overflow with hope through the power of the Holy Spirit.

Day 7: John 14:1 Jesus invites us not to let our hearts be troubled. Our faith in God and in Him provides calm amid worries.

Bishop Vashti Murphy McKenzie

Bishop Vashti Murphy McKenzie is a groundbreaking leader within the African Methodist Episcopal (AME) Church, celebrated for her trailblazing role as the first female bishop in the church's history. Born in 1947, McKenzie has been a powerful advocate for social justice, education, and the empowerment of women throughout her distinguished career. Her leadership is characterized by a profound commitment to faith and a deep reliance on spiritual guidance to overcome challenges. McKenzie has spoken about how her faith has been a source of strength, particularly in managing anxiety and navigating difficult times. She has authored several influential books on leadership, spirituality, and personal growth, sharing her insights and experiences to inspire others. Her work includes initiatives to support education and advocate for marginalized communities, reflecting her dedication to fostering positive change. Bishop McKenzie's journey exemplifies the transformative power of faith and perseverance. By breaking through traditional barriers and embracing her calling with divine support, she has shown how trust in God can turn challenges into opportunities for service and growth. Her life and ministry continue to inspire many, illustrating that with unwavering faith and a steadfast commitment to one's purpose, it is possible to overcome obstacles and achieve lasting impact and fulfillment.

Lord, as we seek Your peace amid our concerns, may our trust in Your plan fill us with calm and strength. Just as Bishop McKenzie found purpose and guidance in You, help us find peace in Your direction and promises. Amen.

Reflective Questions

How can you apply trust in God's plan to calm your anxiety and find peace in the uncertain situations of your life?

....

....

....

....

....

....

....

....

....

How can Bishop Vashti Murphy McKenzie's leadership and faith inspire you to trust in God's plan and seek peace amidst your own challenges?

....

....

....

....

....

....

....

....

Week 50

Embracing God's Guidance

"Your word is a lamp to my feet and a light for my path."
Psalm 119:105

Readings:

Day 1: Proverbs 16:9
Day 2: Isaiah 30:21
Day 3: Psalm 32:8
Day 4: James 1:5
Day 5: Psalm 25:4-5
Day 6: Jeremiah 33:3
Day 7: John 16:13

Week's Reflection

Embracing God's guidance means trusting His direction in our lives. His word illuminates our path, offering clarity and direction amid uncertainty and anxiety.

Reflections

Day 1: Proverbs 16:9 Although we plan our future, it is God who directs our steps. Trusting His guidance ensures that our paths align with His will.

Day 2: Isaiah 30:21 God offers clear direction in every decision. His voice guides our steps, ensuring we follow the right path.

Day 3: Psalm 32:8 God promises to instruct and guide us with His love. His advice is constant and full of care, lighting our way with His wisdom.

Day 4: James 1:5 When we seek wisdom, God generously provides it. His guidance brings clarity in times of doubt and difficulty.

Day 5: Psalm 25:4-5 We ask God to show us His ways and guide us with His truth. Our hope rests in His constant direction.

Day 6: Jeremiah 33:3 God invites us to call upon Him for answers. His revelation provides guidance and understanding in unknown aspects of our lives.

Day 7: John 16:13 The Holy Spirit guides believers into all truth. His direction helps us navigate life, revealing what is yet to come.

Marjorie Stewart Joyner

Marjorie Stewart Joyner was a pioneering African-American entrepreneur whose unwavering faith and visionary spirit profoundly impacted the beauty industry. Born in 1896, Joyner's journey was marked by resilience and dedication. She is best known for inventing the permanent wave machine, a groundbreaking innovation that transformed hair styling for countless women. Her work was driven by a deep-seated belief in divine guidance, which she credited for her ability to overcome significant challenges in a time of widespread racial and gender discrimination. Joyner's success was not merely a testament to her technical skills but also to her profound trust in God. She faced numerous obstacles with grace and determination, believing that her faith provided her with the strength to persevere and innovate. Her contributions extended beyond her inventions; she was a mentor and advocate for other women in the business, using her platform to uplift and empower. Her legacy is a powerful reminder of how embracing divine guidance can lead to transformative achievements and inspire others to follow their dreams with faith and courage.

Lord, as we navigate our own paths, may we be inspired by Marjorie Stewart Joyner's steadfast faith and innovative spirit. Guide us in embracing Your divine direction, as she did, to overcome challenges and achieve our own dreams with courage and purpose. Amen.

Reflective Questions

How can you apply divine guidance in your daily decisions to reduce anxiety and find peace in moments of uncertainty?

....
....
....
....
....
....
....
....
....
....

How can you, like Marjorie Stewart Joyner, find strength and direction through your faith to overcome personal challenges and embrace new opportunities?

....
....
....
....
....
....
....
....154

Week 51
The Power of God's Promises

"The Lord is not slow in keeping his promise, as some understand slowness.
Instead he is patient with you, not wanting anyone to perish, but everyone
to come to repentance."
2 Peter 3:9

Week's Reflection

God's promise is a firm anchor for our lives. His faithfulness and patience assure us that everything He has promised will come to pass, bringing us hope and peace amidst anxiety.

Reflections

Day 1: Hebrews 10:23 God's faithfulness sustains us. By clinging to His hope, we find stability in His promises, regardless of circumstances.

Day 2: Romans 4:20-21 Like Abraham, we can be confident that God will fulfill His promises, strengthening our faith through His power.

Day 3: 2 Corinthians 1:20 Every promise of God is fulfilled in Christ. Our faith and gratitude glorify God and affirm His faithfulness.

Day 4: Psalm 145:13 God is reliable in all His promises. His kingdom and dominion reflect His constant faithfulness through the generations.

Day 5: Isaiah 55:11 God's word always accomplishes its purpose. His promises transform our lives, achieving the goals for which they were sent.

Day 6: 1 Kings 8:56 God has fulfilled His promises to Israel. Every word He has spoken is secure, showing His faithfulness throughout history.

Day 7: 1 Peter 1:4 The inheritance promised by God is eternal. This promise offers us hope and security, preserved in heaven for us.

Dr. Jeanetta Cole

Dr. Jeanetta Cole is a trailblazing educator and civil rights advocate, renowned for her transformative leadership as President of Spelman College from 1987 to 1997. Her deep faith and commitment to spiritual values guided her through the challenges of her tenure, allowing her to lead Spelman to new heights as a premier institution for Black women's education. Under her guidance, Spelman achieved national recognition for its academic excellence and social impact, marked by advancements in curriculum development, institutional growth, and a strong emphasis on social justice and equity. Her dedication to expanding opportunities for marginalized communities has been a cornerstone of her career. Dr. Cole's faith provided a source of strength and resilience, helping her navigate moments of anxiety and difficulty. Her commitment to enhancing educational access and quality for Black women has profoundly influenced educational policies and inspired the next generation of leaders. Beyond her work at Spelman, Cole has been a prominent advocate for civil rights and equity in higher education, driven by her vision of a more just and inclusive society. Her legacy exemplifies how faith-driven leadership and a steadfast dedication to justice can create meaningful and enduring change. Dr. Cole's contributions highlight the power of service and the fulfillment of promises through dedication and advocacy in education and beyond.

Lord, thank You for Your unbreakable promises. Just like Dr. Cole and the heroes of faith, we trust in Your faithfulness to fulfill what You have promised. Strengthen our hope and peace in every challenge. Amen.

Reflective Questions

How can you apply the certainty of God's promises in your daily life to calm anxiety and find peace in moments of uncertainty?

....
....
....
....
....
....
....
....
....

How do Dr. Jeanetta Cole's leadership and faith inspire you to trust in God's promises while facing your own challenges and struggles?

....
....
....
....
....
....
....

Week 52

Building a Legacy of Faith

"One generation commends your works to another; they tell
of your mighty acts."
Psalm 145:4

Readings:

Day 1: Genesis 18:19
Day 2: Deuteronomy 6:6
Day 3: Proverbs 22:6
Day 4: 2 Timothy 1:5
Day 5: Hebrews 11:1
Day 6: Psalm 78:4
Day 7: Matthew 5:14

Week's Reflection

This theme emphasizes the importance of building a legacy of faith that inspires future generations. Our testimony and acts of faith should be passed down and lived out so that the next generation can know and experience God's wonders.

Reflections

Day 1: Genesis 18:19 God's promise to Abraham included a call to guide his family in faith, showing that a spiritual legacy begins at home and is crucial for fulfilling divine promises.

Day 2: Deuteronomy 6:6-7 Passing faith to future generations is an ongoing responsibility. We must teach and model divine values in every aspect of our daily lives.

Day 3: Proverbs 22:6 Instructing children in the Lord's ways is an investment in their spiritual future. Faith nurtured from a young age forms a solid foundation for life.

Day 4: 2 Timothy 1:5 The sincere faith lived by Timothy's grandmother and mother is reflected in him, demonstrating how a family's spiritual heritage can profoundly impact each generation.

Day 5: Hebrews 11:1 Faith gives us confidence in what we hope for and assurance in the unseen. This confidence is shared through personal and communal testimony.

Day 6: Psalm 78:4 Sharing God's deeds and wonders with the next generation strengthens their faith and reminds them of the Lord's faithfulness throughout history.

Day 7: Matthew 5:14 Like a city on a hill, our faith and testimony should shine brightly so that others may see and glorify God.

Esther Rolle

Esther Rolle was a trailblazing actress whose career was marked by both exceptional talent and unwavering faith. Born in 1920 in Pompano Beach, Florida, Rolle overcame numerous barriers to become a prominent figure in the entertainment industry. Her commitment to portraying strong, dignified characters helped redefine how Black women were represented on screen. Rolle is best known for her groundbreaking role as Florida Evans on the TV sitcom Good Times, where she brought depth and respect to her character, challenging stereotypes and advocating for greater accuracy in the portrayal of Black families. Throughout her life, Rolle's deep faith was a source of strength and guidance. She believed in the power of faith to navigate life's obstacles and to build a meaningful career. Her legacy is not only in her pioneering roles but also in her dedication to using her platform to uplift and inspire others. Rolle's story exemplifies how faith can be a cornerstone in building a lasting and impactful legacy. Her courage and belief in a higher purpose continue to inspire women, particularly those navigating their own challenges with resilience.

Lord, as we reflect on Your promise to guide and bless generations, we ask for the strength to build a legacy of faith that inspires and transforms. May our lives be a living testimony of Your greatness and love, just as Dr. Wright's life was in her field. Amen.

Reflective Questions

How can you begin to build a legacy of faith in your own family and community that aligns with the example of the biblical figures you've read about?

....

....

....

....

....

....

....

....

....

.

How can you, like Esther Rolle, draw on your faith to build a meaningful and enduring legacy in your own life?

....

....

....

....

....

....

....

....

Spiritual Goals for Managing Anxiety

Define your spiritual goals with a focus on managing anxiety. Reflect on how you can use this journey to find peace, build resilience, and deepen your connection with God. This section guides you in setting clear intentions to support your mental and spiritual well-being.

- What specific spiritual growth do you seek to alleviate anxiety and strengthen your faith on this journey?

....
....
....
....
....
....
....
....
....
....
....
....
....
....
....
....
....
....

Verses of Calm

These carefully selected Bible verses are designed to be your anchor during moments of anxiety and stress. They offer not just comfort, but a deep sense of peace and reassurance. Turn to these verses whenever you feel overwhelmed, and let their calming words guide you back to a place of inner strength and tranquility.

- Philippians 4:6-7
- 1 Peter 5:7
- Matthew 11:28-30
- Psalm 34:4
- Psalm 46:1-2
- Isaiah 41:10
- Psalm 55:22
- 2 Timothy 1:7
- Romans 15:13
- Psalm 94:19
- John 14:27
- Isaiah 26:3
- Proverbs 12:25
- Psalm 27:1
- Psalm 23:4
- 1 Corinthians 10:13
- Matthew 6:34
- Psalm 118:5
- 1 John 4:18
- Hebrews 13:6

- 2 Corinthians 1:3-4
- Psalm 16:8
- 1 Samuel 12:24
- Colossians 3:15
- Philippians 4:13
- Zephaniah 3:17
- Romans 8:28
- Psalm 37:5
- Psalm 103:13-14
- Isaiah 43:1
- Matthew 6:25-26
- Hebrews 4:16
- Psalm 42:11
- 2 Corinthians 12:9
- Psalm 121:1-2
- Proverbs 3:5-6
- Romans 8:38-39
- Psalm 29:11
- Isaiah 40:31
- John 16:33

Weekly Anxiety Reduction Activities

You'll find practical activities specifically designed to help you manage anxiety effectively. Rooted in spiritual principles and expert research, these challenges offer actionable steps to reduce stress and promote a sense of calm in your daily life.

Week 1

Challenge: Write down three things you are hopeful for and pray for them daily.

Completed: ☐

Week 2

Challenge: Identify one area in your life where you need strength. Journal your thoughts and ask God for help in this area each day.

Completed: ☐

Week 3

Challenge: Create a vision board with your future goals and hopes. Reflect on it each day to remind yourself of God's plans for you.

Completed: ☐

Week 4

Challenge: Choose a fear you want to overcome and take one step towards facing it this week. Share your progress with a friend or mentor.

Completed: ☐

Week 5

Challenge: Find one positive thing in a challenging situation you're facing and write about it. Focus on this aspect each day.

Completed: ☐

Week 6

Challenge: When faced with a decision this week, take time to pray and seek God's wisdom before making a choice. Write down the outcome and your reflections.

Completed: ☐

Week 7

Challenge: Practice a 5-minute daily meditation focusing on God's peace. Record how it affects your thoughts and feelings.

Completed: ☐

Week 8

Challenge: Perform one act of kindness each day for someone in your life. Document each act and reflect on the impact it had.

Completed: ☐

Week 9

Challenge: Write a letter to yourself, acknowledging any emotional wounds and asking for God's healing. Reread the letter at the end of the week and reflect on any changes.

Completed: ☐

Week 10

Challenge: Identify a situation where you need patience. Create a daily affirmation to remind yourself of God's timing and repeat it each day.

Completed: ☐

Week 11

Challenge: List any current uncertainties or challenges. Spend time in prayer each day asking God to guide you and reveal His plan.

Completed: ☐

Week 12

Challenge: Start a gratitude journal and write down three things you are thankful for each day, even in difficult times.

Completed: ☐

Week 13

Challenge: Reflect on a past situation where God's timing was evident. Write about it and how it strengthened your faith.

Completed: ☐

Week 14

Challenge: Identify a current trial and list ways you can build resilience through it. Set small, achievable goals for overcoming it.

Completed: ☐

Week 15

Challenge: Find moments of joy in your daily routine and write them down. Share these moments with someone close to you.

Completed: ☐

Week 16

Challenge: Make a list of things that scare you. Choose one to address this week with a small action and note how it impacts your courage.

Completed: ☐

Week 17

Challenge: Focus on showing love in one specific relationship this week. Observe how it affects the relationship and your own feelings.

Completed: ☐

Week 18

Challenge: Seek wisdom by reading a chapter from Proverbs each day. Reflect on how it applies to your life and decision-making.

Completed: ☐

Week 19

Challenge: Practice an act of compassion each day, such as listening actively or offering help. Reflect on how it affects both you and others.

Completed: ☐

Week 20

Challenge: Identify someone you need to forgive. Write a letter (not necessarily to send) expressing your forgiveness and releasing any resentment.

Completed: ☐

Week 21

Challenge: Take a specific action this week that demonstrates your faith in practice. Document how it impacts your faith journey.

Completed: ☐

Week 22

Challenge: Set aside time each day for quiet reflection in God's presence. Observe how it influences your sense of peace.

Completed: ☐

Week 23

Challenge: Create a list of God's promises from scripture. Choose one to focus on each day and reflect on how it impacts your hope.

Completed: ☐

Week 24

Challenge: Memorize this verse and use it as a daily affirmation for strength. Track how it influences your daily challenges.

Completed: ☐

Week 25

Challenge: Reflect on a current situation where you need patience. Write a daily journal entry about your progress and trust in God's plan.

Completed: ☐

Week 26

Challenge: During a trial, write about how you are experiencing God's strength. Share this with a friend or mentor for support and encouragement.

Completed: ☐

Week 27

Challenge: Spend time each day in activities that bring you joy and acknowledge God's presence in these moments.

Completed: ☐

Week 28

Challenge: Choose one promise from God and reflect on it daily. Write a prayer or affirmation based on this promise.

Completed: ☐

Week 29

Challenge: Seek God's guidance in a specific decision. Write down the process and outcomes of seeking wisdom through prayer and scripture.

Completed: ☐

Week 30

Challenge: Identify a weakness or challenge and focus on how God's grace provides strength. Write about your experiences and growth.

Completed: ☐

Week 31

Challenge: Reflect on a past situation where God's timing was evident. Write a letter to yourself about how this experience has shaped your trust in God's timing.

Completed: ☐

Week 32

Challenge: When faced with a challenge, write down how your faith helps you overcome it. Reflect on your resilience and God's role in it.

Completed: ☐

Week 33

Challenge: Set aside time each day to pray for hope in a specific area of your life. Track any changes in your hope and outlook.

Completed: ☐

Week 34

Challenge: Reflect on a recent provision or blessing from God. Write about it and how it has impacted your trust in God's provision.

Completed: ☐

Week 35

Challenge: Commit to a daily prayer practice for strength. Journal about how it affects your daily life and challenges.

Completed: ☐

Week 36

Challenge: Engage in a creative activity this week and reflect on how it reminds you of God's creativity. Document your experiences and thoughts.

Completed: ☐

Week 37

Challenge: Identify a transition in your life and seek God's guidance. Write down the steps you are taking and how you trust God through the process.

Completed: ☐

Week 38

Challenge: Work on forgiving someone in your life. Write a reflection on how this process affects you and your relationship with the person.

Completed: ☐

Week 39

Challenge: Set a small, achievable goal related to a challenge you're facing. Persevere in working towards it and reflect on your progress.

Completed: ☐

Week 40

Challenge: List the ways God has provided for you recently. Reflect on these provisions with gratitude and joy each day.

Completed: ☐

Week 41

Challenge: Reflect on a time when you experienced God's grace in your life. Write about it and how it has influenced your perspective and actions.

Completed: ☐

Week 42

Challenge: Choose a book of the Bible to read this week. Spend time each day reading and reflecting on it. Write about how it strengthens your faith.

Completed: ☐

Week 43

Challenge: Identify a promise from God that brings you peace. Memorize it and recite it daily, reflecting on its impact on your anxiety or worry.

Completed: ☐

Week 44

Challenge: List a challenge you are currently facing. Write a plan for how you will approach it with courage and faith, and document your progress.

Completed: ☐

Week 45

Challenge: Practice an act of generosity each day. It can be giving time, resources, or support. Reflect on how it affects you and those around you.

Completed: ☐

Week 46

Challenge: Identify three sources of joy in your daily life and focus on them each day. Write about how they impact your overall happiness and outlook.

Completed: ☐

Week 47

Challenge: Track an area where you need provision. Pray about it daily and observe how God provides or guides you in that area. Document your experiences.

Completed: ☐

Week 48

Challenge: When making a decision this week, seek wisdom through prayer and scripture. Write about how seeking God's guidance affects your decision-making process.

Completed: ☐

Week 49

Challenge: Reflect on a current trial and identify how it might be working for your good. Write about your reflections and how this perspective helps you cope.

Completed: ☐

Week 50

Challenge: Start a gratitude journal and write down five things you are grateful for each day. Reflect on how this practice impacts your mood and perspective.

Completed: ☐

Week 51

Challenge: Focus on experiencing and sharing God's love with others. Write about specific ways you've felt God's love and shared it with those around you.

Completed: ☐

Week 52

Challenge: Reflect on the personal growth you've experienced over the past year. Write about the lessons learned, challenges overcome, and how your faith has grown. Celebrate your journey and set new goals for the coming year.

Completed: ☐

Made in United States
Orlando, FL
26 June 2025

62406339R00095